Lightly Salted Stories

Lightly Salted Stories

Copyright © 2013

Martin L. Ramsay

Version 1.1 —December, 2013

Cover design by Tim Pack, Pack Graphics

Published by Narrow Gate House Publishers
1788 Hwy. 1016, Suite C
Berea, Kentucky 40403
www.narrowgatehouse.com

Narrow Gate House Publishers is the publication division of CEATH Company, www.ceath.com.

ISBN # 978-1-941099-00-1

Library of Congress Control Number: 2013923031

lightly salted

Stories

by

Martin Ramsay

Narrow Gate House Publishers

About the Author

Martin Ramsay does not fancy himself to be a writer. He is the Managing Director of CEATH Company, a consulting firm with clients on four continents. In his work, he must take considerable pains to write well, to communicate effectively with his clients, and to help his clients think through the hidden issues that may be obscuring possible strategies. This book is his first attempt at writing fiction and resulted from the need to help others think through some of the foundational assumptions in their own thinking. He found that parables could be helpful in that regard.

Martin lives in Kentucky with his wife of 38 years. They have four grown sons and eight grandchildren. They are active in their local church where Martin is a deacon and teaches adult Sunday School.

Table of Contents

Foreword

I would like to say that this little volume was a labor of love. It was not. It was more a labor of frustration and later a labor of obedience. Allow me to explain.

Seven years ago or so, I was working for a college whose leadership seemed determined to take the institution in a direction that was counter to its historical mission and that would ultimately be destructive for the organization itself and, more importantly, for the students it served. I was not alone in this perspective; many of my colleagues shared my point of view. It was not so much that the leadership of the institution was unwilling to allow us to articulate our perspective, it was that they seemed unable to even consider that a point of view other than their own could be valid. Worse, they seemed unable to see a different perspective; it was as if they were blinded, locked into their own narrow view of the world and unable to broaden their vision. It was a time of deep frustration.

The dialogues—and the use of that term dialogue here is generous, they weren't so much dialogues as exercises in talking "at" each other —that occurred on campus reminded me of the work of Thomas Kuhn on scientific paradigms and the difficulty of seeing a paradigm that is not your own. Kuhn's work was later expanded by Joel Barker in his book, "Paradigms: The

Business of Discovering the Future." In my work as an organizational consultant I had found that Barker's assertions about how our own paradigms can blind us to realities that are right in front of us rang true. That was what seemed to be happening during this time of frustration: the leadership's paradigm was locked into one narrow perspective that led to an inability to see other points of view.

And then a little story came to me. If anything, it was modeled on the stories of Saki (the pen name of H. H. Munro) whose acerbic writing style and twist endings had impressed me as a teenager. I wrote the story down, polished it up a bit, and passed it around to a few of my colleagues. It seemed to me that, through a story—perhaps "parable" is a better word—one could jolt the reader out of his or her paradigm by creating an unfamiliar environment or a challenging situation. This technique might be useful to open up a dialogue that had previously not been possible due to limitations in the reader's paradigms. This could further be enhanced by asking some thought-provoking questions at the end of the story that might further serve to open up dialogue and a vision for other paradigms.

Several more of these little stories came to me in the following months and seemed to be useful for generating discussions about other points of view. I simply started collecting them, not knowing what to do with them.

Then came the labor of obedience. During my quiet time I was impressed again and again that I should "finish the book." I'm a slow learner, but after several years I finally understood that I was to collect these stories (which continued to arrive, unbidden) into a volume. I would like to say that I quickly completed that assignment, but, alas, I was slow in that regard as well. Now, finally, the task is done and the collection of stories you hold in your hand is the result.

My hope is that these stories will be useful. I find that our post-modern world, for all its claims of openness and progressiveness, is surprisingly closed and myopic. Children of the post-modern era grow up with a staggeringly limited perspective; it is very difficult to even consider such paradigm-shattering ideas as absolute truth, the worth of every individual, or the existence of a meta-reality. Perhaps these stories can help. I envision a college professor who is assigned the challenge of a freshman first-year experience course finding them helpful for generating class discussion. The questions to think about at the end of each story could be given as writing or research assignments. Perhaps a youth leader at a church will find them helpful for breaking through the post-modern youth culture. Or perhaps they can help you open up a dialogue about things that have eternal consequences with a friend or family member.

These stories are not overtly Christian. Far from it. In fact, they go out of their way not to be, even though several of them contain Christian themes and all of them are rooted in a Christian perspective that often finds itself in conflict with post-modern myopia. I say this without apology. These parables are designed to be palatable to post-modern people while presenting an alternative paradigm.

There are several people I need to thank. The late Roberta Kells Dorr was a missionary, prolific author, and friend. Even on her death bed, well beyond the ability to speak and with one foot already in Heaven, she squeezed my hand as if to say, "Finish the book. I'm rooting for you." Tim Pack, a pastor and artist, did the cover for me, but, more importantly, over many cups of coffee at the local coffee shop, caught my vision for the book and continued to encourage me. Another pastor and missionary, Bill Vasey of Joyabaj in Quiché, Guatemala also read and provided editorial comments on the book. And one of my lovely daughters-in-law, Maggie Storm Ramsay, served as an outstanding proofreader and editor, all while raising some of the most wonderful grandchildren in the world. The work and contributions of these friends has been invaluable, but responsibility for errors must remain with me. And if you, dear reader, find that the stories challenge, even anger you, I gladly take responsibility for that as well.

Finally, I must thank the woman who has, for the past 35 years, allowed me to be her husband. Charlie is an incredible lady, an outstanding mother and grandmother, and far and away my best friend. She probably has very little idea how simultaneously inspiring and comforting she is to me. This little book is dedicated to her.

And no foreword would be complete without acknowledging the Author of it all. There is no question in my mind that the stories came from Him and, if they have any value at all, it is because He has ordained that it be so. I am merely the obedient vessel who put fingers to keyboard.

Martin Ramsay
Berea, Kentucky
September, 2011

The Train of Tolerance

"Professor Jones!" exclaimed the man in the beard and tweed jacket as he strode along the train platform, suitcase in hand.

"Professor Smith! How marvelous!" wheezed his plump companion, a bit out of breath. He removed his wire-rimmed glasses and wiped the perspiration from his eyes. "Are you on this train?"

"Indeed I am! Going to the conference?" asked Professor Smith.

"Yes, yes." Professor Jones hefted his case up the stairs onto the car. "May I congratulate you, Professor Smith, on your paper on tolerance that was recently published?"

"Thank you my friend." He climbed up behind Professor Jones into the car. "I was quite pleased with it, really. And, by the way, your presentation at the faculty luncheon last week was brilliant. The need for openness on our campus. It was brilliant!"

"Modesty forbids! I was rather pleased, quite pleased with it, though," replied Professor Jones, his round head nodding on his portly frame.

They placed their bags into the overhead rack as they chatted. The car was empty except for an older woman in a faded dress sitting in the far end. She sat quietly reading a tattered book with a zippered leather binding. The men settled into seats opposite each other.

"I did want to ask you about one point on openness." Smith stroked his beard in thought. "It relates to my paper on tolerance. Are you committed to openness everywhere on campus?"

"Of course! Of course!" replied Jones. "In our enlightened age, we must be open to all things. To do anything less is narrow-minded and not worthy of our institution. To do less makes us less human."

"But everywhere?" asked Smith. "I want to probe deeper into how far this openness can reach."

"Without question, Dr. Smith. Would you not agree that complete openness to new ideas is the only way to enlightenment?"

"Indeed I do, Dr. Jones. I couldn't agree more. Your comments were brilliant. The other members of the faculty were equally impressed." H brushed a speck off of his jacket. "I just wanted to make sure I was clear on that point. You see, your thoughts on this reinforce nicely my thoughts in my paper about tolerance. Just as we must be open to all things, we must be completely tolerant. It is the only approach befitting a modern person."

"Yes, yes! Exactly! Tolerance to all ideas, tolerance to all people. I couldn't agree more!" Professor Jones leaned back in his seat as the train lurched and began to move. He stretched his hands out and clasped them behind his head. With a sigh of deep satisfaction he said, "It is marvelous, is it not, to live in such an enlightened time among such enlightened colleagues?"

"Indeed." Professor Smith, too, paused to appreciate their enviable position. "But there are those poor, pathetic creatures out there who are not so enlightened. Narrow-minded bigots, I'd say. They just don't get it, do they? No understanding at all."

They both contemplated this depressing fact as the wheels of the train picked up speed. Suddenly Professor Jones spoke, "I tell you what! Let us declare that this train is, today, a train of openness and tolerance."

"Brilliant! I congratulate you, Professor Jones! An absolutely brilliant idea. This day, at least, in this very place ... this train shall be called the train of tolerance and openness."

They beamed at each other and solemnly shook hands as the countryside slid by. It was a beautiful day with clear blue skies and a sun that bathed the rolling countryside with light. The wheels continued their rhythmic cadence. "Tolerance and openness, tolerance and openness, tolerance and openness." The professors chatted as the next town came into view.

At the next station, a man climbed aboard the car. Luggage was stowed, tickets were duly punched, and seating was arranged. The man was an African-American, in his mid-thirties, with a light tan suit and matching tie. Professor Jones initiated the conversation.

"Good afternoon, sir, and welcome to this train. We have declared this to be the train of tolerance and openness! We welcome you aboard."

"Indeed," echoed Professor Smith. "You are most welcome here. We are open to all, we tolerate all." The lady in the corner glanced at them from over the edge of her spectacles, but said nothing.

"Thank you," said the man. He pulled out a newspaper.

"A glorious day, I tell you, a glorious day!" Jones beamed at the man. "Tolerance and openness, yes sir. Tolerance and openness!"

The train pulled out of the station and continued its journey.

The next stop brought aboard a young woman on crutches. It was obvious from her gait that her legs were malformed. "Ah," said Smith. "Brilliant! We welcome you aboard this train of tolerance and openness." The young woman struggled down the aisle, carefully planting each step in concert with the movement of her crutches.

"Welcome! Welcome!" chimed in Jones. "This is a train where all are welcome, even those who are ... " He struggled to find the correct term. "Ah ... those who are physically challenged."

The woman graced the two men with a half-smile. The black man stood up and helped her settle her belongings. She chose to sit with her back to the two professors.

"You see," said Professor Smith, "We have declared this to be the train of openness and tolerance. We welcome all races." He indicated the black man. "We welcome people with handi ... with physical, ah, challenges." He continued to extol their support of openness and tolerance to the back of her head, while Professor Jones frequently chimed in, adding his considerable intellect to their discourse.

The train slid on across its rails through the late afternoon light.

As twilight approached, the train crossed a large river. "I say," said Jones, looking down at the water. "We must be crossing the state line. The border lies along this river."

"Indeed," said Professor Smith. "We are now in another state. Let us declare that, regardless of the state, this train is the train of tolerance and openness."

"Hear, hear!" Jones was enthusiastic in his support. "We will be open to, will tolerate anything. Anything, I tell you! There is not a biased or prejudiced or judgmental thought on this train!"

"Indeed, not! Brilliant, I tell you, absolutely brilliant!"

The train, having completed its crossing of the river, pulled into another station in the new state.

The next passenger was a young woman with green hair. She was wearing the uniform of her generation: scoop-necked blouse, cut low and short, tight jeans worn low around the hips. She was sporting a butterfly tattoo on her right shoulder and, as she walked toward her seat, the professors caught intriguing glimpses of a dragon tattoo that peeked out from around her waist. Her left ear contained at least a dozen pierced earrings, while her right ear was jauntily connected to a stud through her right nostril via a chain that lay across her cheek.

"Perfect, perfect!" exclaimed Professor Jones. "Our diversity becomes richer!"

"Indeed. You, young person, help us demonstrate our commitment to tolerance and openness. Your choice of dress is quite different from anyone else in this car, and yet we welcome you enthusiastically to our train of tolerance and openness."

The young woman sat across the aisle from the professors. "That's cool, dudes," she said. "That is so cool."

The train sang its lullaby of tolerance and openness as the sun disappeared completely and darkness settled down upon the countryside. Artificial lights came on inside the train. None of the other passengers spoke as Professor Smith and Professor Jones continued their brilliant academic dialogue.

The countryside became more urban as the train passed shops, malls, bars and apartment buildings. At last the train pulled into another station. Streetlights illuminated the platform and the two professors strained their eyes to see who would board next. There was a bit of a delay, then a young man boarded. He was wearing a dark t-shirt and dark glasses. He had a small black beard that matched his jet-black hair.

"Welcome!" chimed Smith. "Welcome to the train of tolerance and openness!"

The man stiffened and looked at the professor through the dark glasses. Something in his demeanor made Smith pause in his usual speech.

Jones was not intimidated. "We have declared that, on this train, there shall be nothing but openness and tolerance. Regardless of race, or religion, or physical handicap, or, or anything else. We welcome all!"

The man in the dark glasses sat in a seat, but he did not settle back. The older woman in the corner glanced up from her reading.

As the train began to move again, all were quiet. The black man read his paper. The woman with the crutches ignored the professors. The young woman with the tattoos and hardware decorations gazed out the window at the neon landscape. The newest passenger sat tensely on the edge of his seat. The professors resumed their colloquy and the woman in the corner said nothing.

Suddenly, the man with the dark glasses was out of his seat. Quick as a cat, he jumped to where Professor Smith sat and, before Smith could react, the man was holding a knife to the professor's throat. "Your money," hissed the man. "I want all of it. Now!" He grabbed his victim's hair and pulled his head back to stretch the neck taut against the blade.

"But, but ..." Smith eyes were wide as he eyed the blade only millimeters from his jugular vein. "I ... I don't ..."

"Tut, tut, Professor Smith!" Jones' voice betrayed a certain nervousness. Whether the tremble in this tone came from concern or fear or righteous indignation at Smith's reaction was difficult, at that moment, to ascertain. "Come, come! This is the train of tolerance and openness! Be open to what the man asks!" The half smile on his lips betrayed his own emotion; he was impatient at his colleague's failure to adhere to the pact of tolerance and openness that had been made.

The man with the knife moved swiftly. He dropped Smith's hair and whirled around, slamming Professor Jones' head back against the headrest and holding the knife to his new victim's chest. "Never mind," he growled. "I don't want your money. I'm going to kill you!"

Jones' reaction could not be described as speech. It was more of a squeak that escaped his flaccid lips.

Smith rubbed his own neck, so recently the object of a knife-edge. "Tolerance and openness." It was almost a whisper. "Be open ... be tolerant ... "

"I don't want to die!" There were visible tears running down Jones' pallid cheeks.

Later, those who discussed the situation from the comfort of their ivied towers decided that the man with the knife must have had his back to the older woman in the corner. And, of course, she must have been masquerading as an older person when, in fact, she was much younger than she appeared. Whatever the circumstances, what happened next could not be denied. One moment the man was holding a knife to Professor Jones' chest. The next moment, the knife went skittering down the aisle as the older woman twisted the man's arm around his back so that he writhed in pain. One moment the man with the knife was in control of the situation; the next moment she was in control of him.

For the first time since their journey began, she spoke. "I have been listening to your drivel all afternoon long. But now, gentlemen, you have crossed the line. Tolerance and openness is all fine when we're talking about people. But tolerance and openness to all ideas and philosophies, to all behavior, is not. This man wants to take your life, sir. Can you tolerate that? Are you open to this behavior?" She pierced Dr. Jones with her eyes even as she twisted his assailant's arm a bit harder, immobilizing him completely.

From deep in Professor Smith's throat came a noise. It wasn't a sound that resembled speech and it certainly wasn't words. It was more of a growl, and it came from deep within him. But it grew louder and louder, and suddenly the growl burst violently from his lips as he sprang to his feet and grabbed the woman by both arms. "No one," he shouted in red-faced anger. "NO ONE will interfere with the tolerance and openness of this train. You cannot be permitted to deny this man his rights!"

The man, now free, backed slowly down the aisle, away from the drama playing out before him. Jones, too, stood up. He regained his breath and shouted, "Professor Smith is right! This is intolerable! You are a judgmental bigot! How dare you tell this man what he can and cannot do?" He opened a window and the night air rushed into the train. Smith bodily picked the woman up—she was not heavy—and carried her to the open window. Together, the two professors stuffed her through. Her body was quickly lost in the darkness as it rolled down an embankment.

"There," pronounced Jones. "Order has been restored." He gasped for breath. "Order has been restored!"

"Indeed it has," said Smith. He turned to his colleague. "May I say that you were brilliant, Professor Jones?"

"Yes, yes, but modesty forbids. I thank you, also, for your role in restoring tolerance and openness to this train." He stooped to pick up the knife where it had fallen. "I believe this is yours," he said to the man with the dark glasses as he handed it to him.

The train sped on through the darkness of night.

Think on These Things

1. What is your reaction to professors Smith and Jones? Are they sympathetic characters? Heroic characters? Flawed characters? Justify your responses.

2. As "The Train of Tolerance" progresses, new characters are introduced as they board the train. List each of the characters and the kind of diversity they bring to the train. Do you know someone who would be uncomfortable interacting with one or more of these types of diversity? Why do you think that is?

3. The term "tolerance" plays a large role in this story. Write your own definition of how the average person would define tolerance. Then look up some definitions of tolerance. Are there different ways in which the word can be taken?

4. Is tolerance a good thing? By what definition of tolerance? Why or why not?

5. Think about the term "absolute tolerance?" How would you define that? Is there such a thing as "absolute tolerance?" What are some of the intellectual difficulties to the concept of "absolute tolerance?"

6. Put yourself in the place of the two professors, first Smith and then Jones, when the man with dark glasses held the knife to their throats. What do you think they were feeling? What was their visceral reaction to

the threat? What was their intellectual reaction? Were there conflicts between those two and, if so, what was the nature of the conflict? How do you think they resolved any conflict they may have been feeling?

7. Think about motives: what were the motives of a) Smith and Jones, b) the man with dark glasses, and c) the woman sitting in the corner? Whose motives are most complex and why?

8. Can you think of examples from today's world in which the term "tolerance" is inadequate to explain the concept it tries to convey? Why is tolerance more complex than it might appear on the surface?

9. What do you think about the ethics of each of the following actions that happened in the story:

   - The man with dark glasses threatening Smith and Jones.
   - The woman in the corner disarming the man with the knife.
   - Smith and Jones removing the woman from the train.
   - Professor Jones handing the knife back to the man with dark glasses.

10. Light and dark are used metaphorically in this story. How are they used? Is the use of light an dark effective? Why or why not?

Judge Bristol Decides

Judge Lana Bristol put her arms through the sleeves and pulled her judicial robes around her. "What's on the docket today, Mr. Handy?"

"Today is the Allman case, your honor. Allman vs. the city of East Reba."

"Oh, right. I remember that one. It has been getting a lot of coverage in the press lately, hasn't it?"

"Yes, your honor. This is the case in which Mr. Allman is suing the city to rescind the ordinance that allows carrying and discharging a hunting weapon on city property."

"Ah, yes." She was now properly attired as befit a judge on the bench. "Tell the bailiff I'm ready." Judge Bristol closed the door of her chambers and walked down the hallway to the courtroom. She heard, muffled through the closed door, the bailiff cry, "All rise!" She paused, assuming an appropriately judicial expression, and entered her courtroom.

It was a larger crowd than usual. She supposed that this case had attracted some attention. After all, it had its controversial elements. The bailiff began his "Hear ye, hear ye" litany as she settled herself on the bench and arranged the various documents in front of her. She folded her hands and looked over the rims of her wire-rimmed spectacles at the crowd that filled the courtroom. She rapped the gavel smartly, intoned the required phrases about court being in session, and asked the courtroom to be seated. "Bailiff, what is our first case today?"

"Case number 1072-38-12, Adam Allman, plaintiff, vs. the city of East Reba."

"Randall Mason, representing Mr. Allman," said the tall man in a conservative suit, sitting at the plaintiff's table. He had risen to his feet as he spoke.

"Thank you, Mr. Mason."

"And James Jacobson for the defense, your honor."

"Hello, Jimmy." Judge Bristol and the city attorney were old friends. "Here dealing with another case against the city?"

"Yes, your honor. And may I say what a pleasure it is to be appearing before you again?"

"Thanks, Jimmy, but let's get on with it, shall we? Mr. Mason, do you wish to make an opening statement?"

"Yes, please, your honor." He stood, acknowledging his client. Adam Allman sat quietly, looking at the table. "Your honor, the city of East Reba has taken a decision with which my client, Mr. Allman, disagrees. The city has decided to grant permission to certain individuals to use hunting weapons on city property to hunt various game. The city contends that this decision is based on compassion for the less fortunate members of our community. The city alleges that the ability to hunt game provides food for the underprivileged. We will show that this is a ruse, that there are larger issues at stake here. We will also show that, by making this move, the city is committing itself to a course that will ultimately be detrimental to East Reba."

"Thank you, Mr. Mason," said Judge Bristol. "Does the defense have an opening statement?"

"Indeed we do, your honor." Mr. Jacobson stood at his place at the defense table. "Mr. Allman suggests some kind of ulterior motive in the city's decision to allow hunting on city property. There is no ulterior motive, only the motive of helping the least fortunate. The prosecution raises the specter of some unnamed future disaster. We shall require proof of this and, of course, none will be found. We expect to quickly show that Mr. Allman's assertions are without merit, even frivolous. And we expect that Your Honor will find for the defense."

"Thank you, Jimmy." The judge settled back in her chair. This was going to be interesting. "Call your first witness, Mr. Mason."

"The prosecution calls Mayor Lawrence."

Mayor Lawrence took the stand and was sworn in.

"Please state your name and position, sir."

The mayor smiled at the lawyers and at the room in general. "Certainly. My name is Shelly Lawrence. I have the privilege of being the mayor of East Reba."

"Thank you, sir. Can you please explain the recent ordinance passed by your administration concerning the use of weapons on city property?"

"Of course. The city was recently made aware of several families within our city limits that are in difficult financial straights. They are having trouble putting enough food on the table and approached the city council and myself about the possibility of allowing them to hunt squirrels and rabbits in the city park. These are families with small children. After much discussion and study, the city council and I decided that this request made sense. Small children deserve to eat, and this decision was about the children. We did not, however, want to discriminate against a specific species or two. So we broadened the language to allow hunting of any species, and we did not limit the kind of weaponry. If a person wanted to hunt with a bow and arrow, for example, he or she would be allowed to do so."

"So this ordinance allows anyone to hunt anything in any place?" asked the defense counsel.

"No, not at all. The hunting is only to take place on city non-residential land. And persons who wish to hunt must fill out an affidavit at city hall certifying that they will hunt in a safe manner. They must also provide proof that they have received proper training in their weapon of choice and that they are entitled to carry that weapon."

"And you see this as a sensible move on the city's part? You see no problems with this ordinance?"

"This is a wonderful choice on the city's part. The children of needy families can now be fed. It is a great and good ordinance." The mayor smiled at the courtroom.

"Thank you, Mayor Lawrence. I have no further questions."

Judge Bristol nodded at the city attorney. "Does the defense wish to cross-examine?"

"Indeed we do, your honor. Thank you. Mayor Lawrence, what is the city's estimate of the number of families that will be served by this ordinance?"

"We had two families approach us originally. We estimate that, at most, six or seven families will ultimately benefit."

"And the children of these families will finally have enough to eat?"

"Exactly."

"Thank you, Mayor. That's all."

"The witness is excused," said the judge. Mayor Lawrence stepped down from the witness box. "Please call your next witness, Mr. Mason."

"The prosecution calls Mr. Adam Allman to the stand."

Mr. Allman stood and walked slowly to the witness stand. "Do you swear to tell the truth, the whole truth, and nothing but the truth, so help you God?" intoned the bailiff.

"I do." Mr. Allman sat.

"Mr. Allman, can you please explain to the court your reasons for bringing this suit against the city?" said Mr. Mason.

"I am convinced that this is a wrong move for the city. It is imperative that it be stopped."

"And why is that, Mr. Mason?"

"There are several reasons. First, there is no precedence for this decision. East Reba has never allowed hunting on public lands before. This will shatter the peace and quiet of our parklands. Second, I am not convinced that the six or seven families estimated by the Mayor are the maximum number of families that will take advantage of this ordinance. I think the actual number is much higher."

"Anything else?"

"Yes. I believe that hunting is wrong. Killing and eating wild game is unbecoming of modern human beings. The fact that it is being done on public land makes it that much more reprehensible."

"Thank you, Mr. Allman. No further questions."

"All-right, Mr. Jacobson. Your turn." Judge Bristol was enjoying this.

"Thank you, your honor." Jimmy Jacobson stepped toward the witness. "Mister Allman." He placed his chin in his hand and shook his head. "Mister Allman. Don't you think this is a bit extreme?"

"Not at all."

"Let me see if I've got this straight. You think this ordinance will destroy peace on public lands, right?"

"That's right."

"That's a bit closed-minded, isn't it, Mr. Allman?"

"Objection!" The prosecution attorney spoke up. "Mr. Jacobson is badgering the witness."

"Overruled. Answer the question, Mr. Allman."

Mr. Allman hesitated. "No," he said quietly. "It isn't closed-minded. It's a fact."

"A fact. Hmmmm. And it is also your assertion that the city has grossly underestimated the number of families that will take advantage of this ordinance."

"It is. The city has done no study, to my knowledge, no survey, to determine the actual number of families who will take advantage of the ordinance and hunt game."

"Have you done any study to the contrary? Can you provide the names of the families that will take advantage of this ordinance beyond the six or seven stipulated by the mayor?"

"Uh ... no, not really. But I am convinced that, when people find out that they can ..."

Jacobson cut him off. "Now, Mr. Allman. You also contend that killing and eating wild game is wrong?"

"Yes, yes I do."

"Tell me, Mr. Allman. Do you eat meat? You know, chicken, beef, and the like?"

"Actually, I'm a vegetarian."

"Ah. So you're trying to force your particular values on the rest of us, is that right?"

"Objection!" The prosecution lawyer was determined. "Mr. Allman's values are not on trial here, your honor."

"No, but he did introduce this line of reasoning in his earlier statement. I'll allow it."

"Thank you, your honor." Jimmy Jacobson was pleased. This was going quite well.

"No, I'm not trying to force my values on others – although I do think killing and eating wild game is wrong. I'm more worried about what this ordinance does to our community in East Reba. We have a wonderful town here. This ordinance may seem innocuous at first. After all, the mayor keeps telling us it is about the children and making sure they have enough to eat. Well, I'm in favor of them having enough to eat. Just not this way. I think this opens the door to a whole bunch of problems that I can only begin to imagine today."

"Care to be specific?" Judge Bristol knew that Jimmy Jacobson was taking a chance by asking the question. The witness could have several sound reasons for his opinions. But, were she in Jimmy's shoes, she probably would have asked the same question. Her hunch was that Mr. Allman's fears were unnamed and unarticulated. The witness didn't disappoint her.

"No, I can't point to a specific thing. But just imagine it – people shooting off guns and other weapons all over the city, supposedly to feed their families, when there are other perfectly good ways to do that. I think it puts us on a very slippery slope."

"I see. So you have these vague, imagined fears about what this will do, and you're willing to deny food to poor children to do it. Is that right?"

"Objection! Your honor, please ..."

"Withdrawn!" The city attorney had gotten his point in. "I'm through with this witness."

Both sides called several other witnesses. The prosecution called a witness on noise levels of various firearms and on the dangers of stray ammunition. The defense called an expert on child poverty and hunger who was particularly articulate in describing the plight of East Reba's poorer families. But the major points had already been made. It boiled down to a difference in point of view, and Judge Bristol was very clear on the differences. On one side was the desire to help children who needed help, on the other, a vague fear about where this might lead. Perhaps she suffered from a failure of imagination, but the Judge just couldn't see how Mr. Allman's arguments held water.

The defense rested. Judge Bristol banged her gavel and stated, "Court will take a thirty minute recess to consider the matter."

She stood up. "All rise!" bawled the bailiff. Judge Bristol returned to her chambers.

It was not a difficult decision. She reviewed the testimonies of the witnesses, but found little to support the prosecution's assertions. She drank a cup of coffee and checked her e-mail. Then she notified her clerk to reassemble the court.

Settled once again on her bench, she looked directly at Mr. Allman. "Mr. Allman had brought an interesting suit to this court. He suggests that the city's new ordinance, designed to provide food for needy families – at no expense to the city, I might add – has some unnamed problems associated with it. He raises the specter of some future horror and talks of East Reba now being on some kind of slippery slope. Mr. Allman, I want to ask you a question, point blank. What are you afraid of? Just what is it that you are afraid of?"

Mr. Allman did not speak. He met the judge's gaze steadily, but made no response.

"The court finds in favor of the defense. Mr. Allman's suit is dismissed. And," she said, as she gave the gavel a resounding thump, "We're adjourned."

Two years had passed since the verdict in his lawsuit against the city. Adam Allman sat at breakfast with his wife, eating toast with strawberry jam and reading the paper. The headlines were, again, very disturbing. This time, a young teen had been killed by a stray bullet. The theory was that this was a gang shootout gone awry. There certainly had been a lot of gunplay that day in the park. No one seemed to notice that the object of the bullets had shifted from squirrels and rabbits to other people. No one seemed to notice that the number of people carrying and using guns had risen dramatically in the past two years. But

Mr. Allman did. He read each morning's headlines with increasing dismay.

"They're at it again," he said to Mrs. Allman.

"Who is at what, dear?"

"More guns, more shooting, more killing. A young man was killed again last night."

"Dear, dear. It isn't safe to go out any more."

"No, it isn't," said Mr. Allman grimly. "But out I must go."

He kissed his wife on the cheek and headed out to work.

His route took him through the city park. He heard the gunfire before he actually saw several people with their guns. It sounded like a Fourth of July fireworks display – the concussions of the explosions were frequent and all around. He heard bullets whizzing overhead and dove behind a dumpster.

His first concern was for his own safety, even as he realized that some of the bullets were actually hitting the metal walls of the dumpster. He tried to make himself small. It was only then that he saw there was another person seeking shelter in the same place. It was a woman. She had her back to him and was peeking around the other side of the dumpster.

"Careful!" he whispered. "Don't let them see you! You'll become a target if you do. I've been in this situation before. It is best if you just lay low until the shooting dies down."

The woman turned around and looked at him. At first he didn't recognize her without her judicial robes wrapped around her. But there could be no doubt: it was Judge Bristol.

At first, Adam Allman couldn't think of what to say. This was a poignant moment, so fraught with danger and irony. The judge didn't speak, she only looked around the side of the dumpster again.

"Judge Bristol, in your courtroom, you asked me a question which I did not know how to answer," he whispered. "You asked me what I was afraid of. Well, now I know. This, this is what I was afraid of. I couldn't articulate it then, but I can show it to you now. I'm afraid of people carrying guns everywhere. I'm afraid of people using their guns whenever they feel like it. I'm afraid of what this has done to East Reba."

A fresh volley of bullets his the dumpster and whined overhead.

"I wish it were in my power to set back the clock to a time before the ordinance," he said. "I would do a better job of explaining why this was a horrible road for our town. I tried the best I could with what I was able to say at the time. I still think it was right to bring suit agains the city in court. But your court found against me, Judge Bristol. Do you think I was wrong?"

The judge turned to look at him again. It was only then that he saw the gun in her hand. The bullets continued to spray around them.

Think on These Things

1. Obtain a copy of the Constitution of the United States of America. What specifically does the Second Amendment say that applies to the subject of this story? In what ways has the Second Amendment been interpreted differently by different courts and groups?

2. In the story, "Judge Bristol Decides," there are two opposing points of view that come out in the scene in the courtroom. Describe the arguments for and against both points of view. In what ways could you strengthen the arguments on both sides?

3. With which of the two sides do you find yourself most aligned? Describe why you take the side you do, and back up your choice with a well-reasoned argument.

4. In the story, Adam Allman finds himself unable to articulate clearly why he thinks allowing hunting in the park is a bad idea. Have you ever found yourself in a situation where a group of people thought one way, and you thought another, but you couldn't quite provide a convincing rationale for your stance? What happened? Did it turn out that you were right after all? Or did the crowd know better? Is the majority always right?

5. What happens at the end of the story that implies that Adam Allman may have been correct in his fears, even though he stated

them poorly in court? As you were reading the first part of the story, did you think that is how it would end? Why or why not?

6. Can you think of major issues in modern society (other than the use of firearms to hunt wild animals) in which people hold dissenting points of view? There are many examples to choose from, but select an issue in which the choices made by society as a whole will have far-reaching consequences. Describe the issue and then describe the arguments for and against both sides of the argument. On which side do you stand? Why is that?

7. In the story, Adam Allman's fears ended up being realized by the escalating violence and killings the city experienced. Yet he could not, in the courtroom, precisely define what he was afraid of and how his fears might play out. Using your example issue from question six, what might be the far-reaching consequences for society that you can imagine? Describe a future in which your fears are realized. What steps need to be taken now to ensure that this future scenario does not come to pass?

8. In the story, Judge Bristol sits on the bench in a courtroom. What words would you use to describe how a judge is to behave? It may be useful to look up some definitions of "judge." Is the word "impartial" on your list? Do you think a judge should be impartial? Why or why not? Do you think Judge Bristol

is impartial? Why or why not? Do you think it is possible for a judge, or anyone else, to be truly impartial? Why or why not?

Mallory Springs

"Is that you, Elizabeth?" Aunt Emma leveraged her aging bones up out of the chair and moved toward the door. The shadow falling across the front room window sheers in the late afternoon sun looked like Elizabeth's profile. She opened the door and held open the screen. "It is you, Elizabeth. Come in, come in! Before you freez to death out there."

Elizabeth's face was pale and drawn. "Oh, Aunt Emma. I'm so glad you're home."

"Why, where else would I be? It's just me an' Old Tom." She glanced over at the large tabby curled up by the wood stove. The cat deigned to open one eye to inspect the visitor, then went back to his feline dreams.

"I really need to talk to you, Aunt Emma."

"That's fine. Jus' fine. Let me put on a pot of coffee." She ushered the younger woman into her small room. "Skinny as a rail," thought Emma as she closed the door against the winter cold. "Bless her heart. She'd still be skinny if she stood beside herself."

Elizabeth walked into the familiar room. To call it humble would be generous. The floors were plank that, at one time, had been covered with a roll of linoleum. But the linoleum had worn through in many places, revealing the chestnut boards underneath. "How long has this house been here," Elizabeth wondered. "I know Aunt Emma's daddy was born in this house, so it has to be 100 years old, at least."

There was an odor to the house – not a bad smell, but a distinctive one. It was a redolent mixture of wood smoke from the stove, yesterday's meal of green beans cooked with fat back and cornbread, and age. Elizabeth was familiar with the path to the outhouse out the back kitchen door – it wasn't that kind of smell. She had visited here often as a young girl and the odor of the house brought back memories, pleasant memories of Jack Tales told by firelight on long summer's nights, of cranking ice cream on the back porch, of running in the woods and getting her knees scraped and Aunt Emma putting mercurochrome on them. Some folks, she supposed, wouldn't find the smell of Aunt Emma's house pleasant, but she did. It was the smell of home, the smell of family and memory. It was the smell of wisdom.

Emma still ground her coffee with an old hand grinder and she perked it the old way. She put the grounds in the basket and filled the percolator with water and set it on the top of the wood stove. Elizabeth heard it hiss as the water droplets on the outside touched the hot surface of the stove. "Sit down, girl, sit down. Take yer coat off. The coffee'll be ready in two shakes of a lamb's tail."

Elizabeth realized she was still standing in the middle of the room. She took off her coat and laid it on the back of the old couch. For a moment she saw herself with her long blonde hair unbound, sitting on that couch, with two of her cousins, laughing and telling tales to each other as kids will do. Her heart ached as she sat down.

"Now what's troubling you, girl?" Aunt Emma lowered herself into her rocker – the one she always sat in, facing the wood stove and the old black and white TV that only picked up three stations, and that was on a good day when the sky was clear. Her hand rested briefly on the large print Bible lying on the side table next to her. She looked over at her niece, hunched on the couch across from her.

She waited.

Eventually Elizabeth spoke. "I've just come from the doctor." Emma knew, even without Elizabeth having to tell her. "Hit's cancer," said Elizabeth, and suddenly tears welled up in her eyes and she couldn't speak again.

"There, there, girl." There was silence in the room for a moment, broken only by the hiss of the wood stove, the percolator just beginning to boil, and the tick-tick-tick of the old mantle clock on the shelf above the stove. "What did the ole' doctor say?"

"Hit's terminal." Elizabeth almost whispered. "He says they ain't much they can do." She swallowed and tried to regain her composure. "Oh, Aunt Emma. What am I going to do? I don't want to ..." Her voice trailed off and she couldn't bring herself to say the final word.

Emma heaved herself up out of her rocker and gathered together the coffee cups and saucers. She poured a cup for herself and one for Elizabeth, setting it on the side table where Elizabeth could reach it easily. "I'm real sorry to hear that, sweetheart." She settled back into the chair and sipped the hot, strong liquid. "Don't they give any hope a'tall?"

"Well," Elizabeth squirmed at the thought. "They say they can take off both breasts." If it was possible, she became even more pale at the thought of such a radical procedure. "But even then, they say my chances ain't good."

"Hmmph!" The old woman pondered a bit, recalling a time many years ago.

"What'll I do, Aunt Emma? James can't do for himself. He don't know how to cook, nor clean, nor nothin'. He's a good provider. He's taken care of me all these years, but he depends on me to keep house and keep him fed. And then there's that sorry son of mine. How I raised a young'un like that I'll never know. Can't hold a job – just about useless. Got that Missy pregnant and won't marry her. And now there's little Brandon. He gets packed back and forth from house to house. I reckon his mam-maw is the only stability in that child's life.

When he comes to stay with me, he behaves and he eats good and – I declare, I don't know what would happen to that young'un if something happened to me. They's people that depend on me, Aunt Emma. Don't you see? I can't die!" She looked at Emma with a fierceness as if she was challenging the older lady to fix it, fix it right that minute.

"Let me tell you a story, girl." The old woman took another sip of her coffee. "Hit's a story from a long time ago." She paused a moment, remembering back, gathering her thoughts like a skein of yarn that had gotten tangled up and needed to be put right.

"You may not know this, but I had cancer once." She saw Elizabeth stiffen. "In the breast, just like you. The doctors told me they weren't no hope." She opened the drawer in the side table and fished around for a piece of paper. It was in an old envelope, now faded with age. She handed it across to Elizabeth. "Read that."

Elizabeth looked at the letter. It had been addressed to Emma using a typewriter. It looked old fashioned now. The return address was a doctor's office in Lexington. She pulled out the single sheet of paper, done with the same typewriter font on letterhead from the doctor's office. It was a short letter, and she immediately grasped its meaning. "Cancer," it said. "Terminal. Nothing we can do. No hope." These were words she had heard just hours ago herself. She looked over at Aunt Emma. "You, too?"

"Yes, honey," said Emma. "Me too. I know what you're going through."

"But ... you're still here? What did you do?"

"Well, Elizabeth, you've come to me for advice, so I'm going to tell you. They ain't too many people will believe what I'm about to tell you, but hit's the Gospel truth.

"Some 40 years ago, I had cancer." She pointed to the letter still in Elizabeth's hand. "They said they weren't no hope, that I had less than two months to live. But I'm here to tell you, I'm a walkin' miracle."

Elizabeth sat forward on the couch.

"You've heard me tell about Mallory Springs?" Elizabeth nodded. It was one of the fabled places of the stories that had been told on those long summer evenings when she and her cousins had been allowed to spend the night with Aunt Emma.

"Well, Elizabeth, the waters of Mallory Springs have the power to cure. I'm here to tell you, because I drank from the waters of Mallory Springs, my cancer was healed."

Elizabeth started in disbelief. "I thought Mallory Springs was just a tale you told us when we were kids."

"No, girl, hit's real all right. And I'm the living proof." She waved her old, worn hands in the air.

"But it can't be, Aunt Emma. You're telling me that just drinking from a spring can cure cancer."

"Yes, girl, that's what I'm a-tellin' you. Mallory Springs has the power to cure. Don't you want to go get some?"

Elizabeth's eyes were large and some of the color was coming back into her face. "Mallory Springs is a real place? Where is it?"

"Why, hit's over at the base of Pilot Knob Mountain. They ain't many folks any more know where it is. You have to go searching for it. Hit's up a narrow path, way off the main road out Red Lick. But I'm a-tellin' you, hit's worth the trip." She paused and looked full on the thin woman sitting across from her. "Do you want to go? I'll take you."

Elizabeth sat back against the couch back. Emma watched the range of emotions cascade across her face. Fear. Anguish. Despair. Hope. Expectation. Doubt. Disbelief. "You can't be serious." Elizabeth's voice was controlled and quiet. "There is no way that water from an old mountain spring can cure cancer. Just no way."

"I'm a-tellin' you, hit's the Gospel truth."

"Aunt Emma, I mean no disrespect. But science has come a long way in 40 years. There must be some other explanation. Or you were one of the fortunate few. But water from a spring? I'm sorry, Aunt Emma. I just don't believe it."

"What can I tell you, girl? You came to me for advice, and I'm giving it to you. I'm telling you to go drink from the waters of Mallory Springs."

Elizabeth suddenly stood up, grabbing for her coat. "No. It just doesn't make sense. It can't be."

Aunt Emma almost whispered, "What can it hurt to believe?"

"No." Then, with more conviction: "NO! I've got to go find someone who can help me."

"But, girl," whispered Aunt Emma. "You've still got the cancer in you."

"I know, I know, Aunt Emma." Her voice was wild, tinged with panic. "I've got to find someone who can really help me."

"I'm a-tellin' you, Elizabeth. Drink from the waters of Mallory Springs. Hit'll cure your cancer. I know."

But Elizabeth wasn't hearing any of that. She wrestled with her coat and headed out the door as Emma was struggling out of her rocker.

"Goodbye, Aunt Emma," Elizabeth's voice was a barely controlled shriek as she crossed the porch and went down the steps. Emma opened the screen door and watched her lope to her car.

"Hurry back, girl! I'll take you to Mallory Springs whenever you want to go."

She watched Elizabeth back her car around in the yard and head down the muddy road that led up to Emma's house.

"Lord a'mercy!" she breathed. "Lord, give her another chance. Just give her another chance." She patted the font of her sweater. They weren't quite as full as they were 40 years ago, but they were still healthy. "And they're still here," she whispered to no one in particular. "And I'm still here."

She pulled on her overcoat and got her walking cane from behind the door. "Come on, Tom," she said to the cat, who was watching her with one open eye. "I feel the need to walk up to Mallory Springs." She grabbed the rail of the steps next to the porch and eased herself down. "Hit's several miles, all right. But the walk will do us both good."

Think on These Things

1. There are only two characters in this story (if you don't count the Old Tom). Imagine Elizabeth's feelings as she is pulling up the driveway to Aunt Emma's house. What would have motivated her to visit Aunt Emma today? What do you think she expected to happen as a result of her visit to Aunt Emma?

2. How do you think Emma felt about Elizabeth's news? Why would she have felt this way? Do you think she was glad that Elizabeth came to her, or would she have preferred that Elizabeth hadn't come? Why do you think that?

3. From the small bits of information provided, what do you think life is like for Aunt Emma at the current stage in her life? What occupies her time? What do you think she thinks about when she is alone?

4. What do you know about Elizabeth's life? What can you extrapolate about what her life must be like? How do you think she feels about her husband? How does she feel about her son? How does she feel about her grandchild?

5. What is Elizabeth's reaction to the news that she has cancer? She seems afraid of something in the story – what is it? What about the cancer worries her most? Why?

6. What do you think about Aunt Emma's claim that the water of Mallory Springs cured her cancer? Is she telling the truth? Is she mistaken? Could it be true? Explain your answers.

7. Have you ever known someone who had a disease that, according to the medical doctors, could not be cured – but they were cured anyway? If you don't know someone, ask some of your friends if they do. What happened? Were the doctors wrong; or was there a more miraculous explanation needed?

8. Can you think of things that science can't explain adequately? How do you feel about that? Is there something beyond science? If so, what is it? Write down some thoughts about the relationship between science and the things that may be beyond science.

9. Suppose, for a moment, that Aunt Emma's explanation of how her cancer was healed is exactly correct – that the waters of Mallory Springs have the power to cure cancer. What responsibility does Aunt Emma have, if any, to force Elizabeth to drink from the waters of Mallory Springs? Should she have been more forceful with Elizabeth? What should she have done differently?

10.If the waters of Mallory Springs really do cure cancer, Elizabeth is clearly being foolish for ignoring Aunt Emma's advice. Can you think of situations where people have ignored good advice? What happened? What might motivate someone to ignore such advice?

What responsibility do people have for the results of their actions when they ignore good advice?

New Math

King Leopold looked out over his courtiers and smiled. He was in an expansive mood; there was peace in his kingdom, trade was reasonably prosperous, and his subjects were reasonably loyal. He settled back into his throne, a remarkably comfortable piece of furniture, for all its splendor and regal symbolism. "What is next on our agenda, Master Wells?" he enquired of his master-at-arms. Today was Wednesday, the day in which commoners were allowed to approach the royal court.

King Leopold enjoyed Wednesdays. Unlike his father before him, he liked being among his subjects. Of course they were complimentary to him; he was king, after all, wasn't he? But they seemed to genuinely appreciate his rule. It was well known that anyone in the kingdom, from a well-placed courtier to the poorest serf, could bring his petition to the royal court and get a fair hearing. Leopold's court was that open-minded, that progressive. As he waited for the master-at-arms to locate the next item on the docket, Leopold lapsed into reverie. "What if," he mused to himself, "What if I were to became known as Leopold the Open? Or, perhaps, Leopold the Tolerant? Would that not be a legacy to leave?"

His reverie was interrupted by the master-at-arms. "If it please your majesty," he announced with a voice that carried to the far corners of the gilded throne room, "The court is being petitioned by two masters from the university to hear their new theory of mathematics."

"Mmmmm ..." Leopold was unenthusiastic. Could be interesting; could be very boring. "Very well. Approach."

"His Excellency, King Leopold, will hear the case of Professor Boyd and Professor Lobin. Step forward!" Two bearded men in academic regalia stepped forward, snatching their ludicrous caps from their bald heads and setting up a small wind from the flapping of the sleeves on their gowns. "Thank you, thank you, your majesty," they said, almost in unison. "We are humbled by your willingness to hear us." They bowed low before the throne on its raised dais.

"Yes, yes. State your case, pray." The king sat with his chin propped on a hand propped up by an elbow propped on the arm of his throne. "Something about mathematics, I believe?"

"Indeed, your majesty. A new kind of mathematics!" The one on the left spoke first. The king was unsure – perhaps uninterested is more accurate – about which one was Boyd and which one was Lobin.

"Pray explain yourselves."

"It is quite simple, your majesty. Modesty forbids us from saying it is brilliant." The one of the right was speaking now. "But quite simple and so enchanting."

"A new mathematics, majesty!" The one on the left echoed his brother academic. "An opportunity for your kingdom to be the first to embrace this bold new approach!"

"A bold new approach! Majesty, your kingdom can show its progressiveness ..."

"Your majesty can show his open-mindedness to new ideas ..."

"New ideas!"

While he found their mannerisms vaguely annoying, the king was intrigued by an idea which might further his reputation for open-minded progressiveness. He tried not to show it, however. It wouldn't do to let his subjects see his interest. "Please explain your new mathematics, professors."

"It is quite simple, majesty ..."

"Quite simple!"

"You see, most mathematicians base their work on the assumption that a number can have only one value. Very closed-minded of them, don't you think?"

"Closed-minded!"

"Most people assume that the only possible value of the number two is, well, two!" He held up two fingers and his colleague, to demonstrate, counted them: "One. Two!"

"However," the other continued, "The number two, when spelled, has three letters." He held up three fingers, and the other professor counted them: one, two, three. He spelled as he counted, "T. W. O."

"The number four has four letters – F O U R. But the number five also has four letters – F I V E!"

"Do you see the possibilities, majesty? This opens up so many more options!"

"Many more options!"

"In short, your majesty, a number need not have only one value. Not at all!"

"Not at all!"

"There is so much potential, here, once we have broken the old-fashioned strictures of the past. This new mathematics will open up huge new vistas for scientific inquiry, for exploration, for commerce ... the list goes on and on."

"On and on!"

"Hmmmm ..." Leopold was intrigued. "So two plus two could equal four, if done the old way, but it could also equal six – T W O plus T W O is six letters." He held up both hands, each with three fingers extended.

"Precisely, your majesty!"

"Brilliant!" The professors were positively beaming.

"I see," said the king. "Three could be three, but it could also be five. Five can be three or four! Six can be six ... or three!" The king beamed at the professors who were nodding their heads so enthusiastically that their beards rippled in waves down their respective chests.

"See, I told you, Dr. Boyd!" said the one on the right. "Our king is, indeed, very intelligent and capable of understanding new ideas." He said it sotto voce, but the entire court could hear him.

Leopold smiled. It was not an obvious attempt at flattery, and it rang true. He was pleased, both with the work of the professors and with his own ability to grasp their new ideas. Perhaps most importantly, he was pleased with the opportunity this presented to further his agenda for the kingdom: embracing this new idea would certainly enhance its reputation for its progressive open-mindedness.

King Leopold cleared his throat and spoke with the gravity that the situation required. "We have considered this matter," he announced. "We have found the idea proposed by these professors to be highly meritorious. Therefore, be it known that henceforth ... are you getting this, Master Wilson?"

"Oh, yes sir, every word!" The Royal Secretary had quill in hand and was carefully transcribing the king's words onto parchment.

"Henceforth, numbers may have multiple values. They may have a value based on their numerical equivalent. Or they may have a value based on the number of letters in their spelled name. This decree has been made by His Excellency, King Leopold ... et cetera, et cetera ... you know what to put, Master Wilson ... to further the progressive open-mindedness of this kingdom. Signed, by my hand this day ... fill in the rest, Master Wilson."

The Royal Secretary finished with a flourish of his quill, and brought the parchment over for the king's examination. Leopold checked it over carefully, then affixed his seal to it. "Very good, Master Wilson. See to it that the Royal Criers spread this decree throughout the kingdom as quickly as possible."

He then turned to the two professors who were all but quivering with excitement. "Gentlemen, we are appreciative of this fine work you have done. We are awarding you the Medal of Academic Valor. This is a new award we have just established for this auspicious occasion. You will be invited to a royal banquet in the near future to be honored with this award." He glanced over at Master Wilson. "See to it, will you, Wilson? And now, gentleman, the court wishes you a good-day. We look forward with anticipation to see what bold and new affects this new decree will have on our splendid kingdom"

The Professors Boyd and Lobin were effusive in their obsequious thanks, in their unctuous smiles, in their quivering bowing and scraping, in their exit – which could almost be described as skipping down the carpet which lead from the throne to the great gilded doors of the royal hall.

The new mathematics decreed by the king did not take hold as quickly as he would have liked.

"Wilson!" he roared one Tuesday. "Why has our new decree not gone into effect?"

"If it please your majesty, the people are having a hard time adjusting to the new ways of thinking. But I am given to understand through my sources that some of the people are trying to … to experiment with the new concept."

"They need to try harder!"

"Perhaps, Majesty, the people need more time."

"Hmmmph! We expect our decrees to be implemented more promptly!"

Weeks came and went, and the new idea did, indeed, appear to be taking hold. Professors Boyd and Lobin returned to court to accept their medals and to report on the glorious experiments that were being undertaken by the populace. "It is very gratifying," said Boyd, "To see such openness, such willingness to embrace the future."

"Gratifying, indeed," echoed Lobin.

One Wednesday, several months after the initial decree, found King Leopold on his throne, receiving petitioners in the throne room. A pair of tradesmen approached, one apparently was a baker, for he still had the white flour dust on his apron and hat. Master Wells, the master-at-arms, announced, "Mr. Samuel, the baker, has a complaint against Mr. Zloff. He claims that Mr. Zloff cheated him out of the full price for a loaf of bread."

"How tedious," thought Leopold to himself. "Approach! Mr. Samuel, is it? What seems to be the problem?"

"May it please the king, this man" – he indicated Mr. Zloff – "Is endeavoring to cheat me out of the price of a loaf of bread. Everyone knows that the price of a loaf of bread is six coppers. Yet, when I sold a loaf to Mr. Zloff this morning, he only paid me three and insisted this was enough! He will pay no more, although I suspect by now my bread has been eaten. I have been cheated out of my rightful price!"

"Tut, tut," said the king. "Our court will not tolerate cheaters. What have you to say for yourself, Mr. Zloff?"

"Majesty, I only wish to follow your wonderful decree. Mr. Samuel charges six coppers for his bread, as do most bakers. But, based on your majesty's new methods of counting, I should pay three coppers for the bread, since the word 'six' has but three letters in it." He glanced triumphantly at the baker.

"But majesty!" The king cut the baker off with a wave of his hand.

"Mr. Zloff has a point! Six does have but three letters. The decree specifically allows this kind of transaction. Mr. Samuel, you must obey the decree on pain of punishment."

"But majesty, the price of flour ... I can scarce afford ..."

"Quiet!" roared the king. "The decrees of the king are above reproach! However, some compromise must be reached." He put his chin in his hand a closed his eyes. Suddenly, a brilliant idea formed in his mind.

"Mr. Samuel, you ordinarily charge six coppers for a loaf of bread, is that right?"

"Yes, majesty, as do all bakers in your kingdom. But, still ..." He stopped as he saw the stormy look on the king's face.

Leopold turned to Mr. Zloff. "And you, sir. You are prepared to follow the new decree about the alternative way of using numbers?"

"I am, your majesty, with all my heart!"

"Good. Now, Mr. Samuel, I recommend that you reduce your price for a loaf of bread to five coppers. Then Mr. Zloff will pay you four, since the word 'five' has four letters. In doing so, you will have gained a copper, and Mr. Zloff will be following my decrees to the letter. Is that understood?" The king glanced at the Royal Secretary who had a secret smile on his face. That Mr. Wilson recognized the king's brilliance in this solution was quite obvious.

"Yes, your majesty." Mr. Zloff was not happy about paying an extra copper, but it was a clever solution.

"Yes, your majesty," said Mr. Samuel, without enthusiasm. He was mentally calculating the cost of baking a loaf of bread. The ingredients alone cost close to four coppers per loaf. On top of that, he had to buy wood for the oven and pay his helper. Under the king's decree, he would loose money on every loaf and soon be out of business. But he was a pragmatic man and he backed out of the throne room, bowing to the king as he went. Perhaps he could use the new mathematics to his own advantage with the miller who supplied his flour.

The case of Samuel vs. Zloff was only the first of what turned out to be a large number of disagreements over prices and quantities. Leopold was able to display his openness, his fairness, and his cleverness as he worked out compromises and verdicts to keep the peace and move the country toward its open-minded destiny. The king found the whole experience invigorating. He was displaying to his people his own ability to rule over them in an open-minded way. 'Leopold the Wise' was beginning to have a certain quality, a certain ring to it.

The last case of the day was from a soldier, a young recruit by the look of him. "Sergeant Kroff of the Royal Armory," announced the master-at-arms. "Step forward!"

"We see from your uniform that you are a member of the Royal Army, is that not true, Sergeant?"

"I am, your majesty, in the Royal Armory. I am attached to the squadron at the Royal Munitions Depot. We are responsible for maintaining your majesty's supply of weapons and gunpowder."

"For which we are very grateful, to be sure. What brings you to our court today, Sergeant?"

"I was sent, your majesty, by my superior officer, Captain Daeveze, to obtain a ruling from the royal court. I am here to state the facts as carefully as I am able, and to ask that your majesty guide your humble servants in our work at the Munitions Depot."

"Very well, Sergeant. State your case."

"Majesty, the Munitions Depot is a carefully run operation. We follow rules and procedures to ensure the effectiveness of your majesty's munitions, and to ensure the safety of your majesty's subjects."

"Very commendable, indeed."

"Majesty, as you know, we manufacture a variety of munitions for use by the army. Everything we do is governed by our Royal Army Rulebook. The Rulebook includes, for example, the quantity of gunpowder to load in a cannon before firing."

"Yes, of course it does. Pray, continue."

"This morning we came across a formulary for a certain type of cannon. The Rulebook calls for one point five standard scoops of gunpowder to be used." He paused to see if the king wanted him to continue. The king made no response, so Sergeant Kroff plunged ahead. "Captain Daeveze pointed out to us men that under your majesty's new decree, we should put seven scoops of gunpowder in. The captain's thinking is that 'one' has three letters and 'five' has four, making a total of seven."

"Quite right," said the king. "So where is the problem?"

"Well, your majesty, Master Sergeant Gulliver pointed out that the word 'point' – as in 'one point five' – has five letters. Master Sergeant Gulliver proposed to Captain Daeveze that the correct amount of gunpowder was twelve scoops – three for 'one,' five for 'point,' and four for 'five.' There was much discussion among the men, your majesty, and Captain Daeveze sent me to obtain, if your majesty will, a ruling on whether or not we should count the letters in the word 'point.' Captain Daeveze said that he would proceed with seven scoops until he received word from the royal court."

"You did right, Sergeant, and your Captain did as well, by sending a representative to the court. We are to decide such matters. We did anticipate, indeed our professors predicted, that this new open-minded mathematics would prompt additional questions and inquiry. Your have brought us such a challenge today, and for that we are grateful. This provides our subjects with the opportunity to see how open-minded we can be, how progressive we are in this kingdom ..."

He did not get to finish his speech, for it was interrupted with a very loud thud that shook the walls of the palace, vibrating even the king where he sat. The indescribable boom was echoed off the palace walls, creating the effect of a wall of sound passing through the throne room again and again. Many covered their ears and huddled towards the corners. One of the female courtiers screamed and promptly fainted. A tapestry, jarred loose by the sound, came hurtling down the wall, burying two courtiers in its folds.

"Mr. Wilson," the king bellowed, attempting to be heard above the spreading panic in the court. "Step to the window and discern the origins of that sound!"

Mr. Wilson was instantly at the window, shading his eyes from the afternoon sun, and scanning the rooftops of the village. "It appears to have come from the direction of the Royal Armory, your majesty. I see a large cloud of smoke in the air over the munitions depot. I would hazard to say a large explosion has occurred, your majesty."

The panic among the court was spreading, with people squeezing past each other to get out of the door as quickly as possible. "Calm yourselves! Calm yourselves! Your king commands it!" shouted Leopold above the din. But it was to no avail. He joined Wilson at the window as the panic swirled around him. "Can you determine what caused it?"

"No, majesty, I cannot. I see now that the armory is engulfed in flames. If I may hazard a guess ..."

"By all means, Mr. Wilson."

"Majesty, I would venture to say a very large explosion has occurred at the armory because a cannon was loaded with much too much gunpowder."

"Stuff and nonsense," replied the king. "My soldiers know what they are doing. They are simply obeying their king's new decree. The idea of including five scoops for the 'point' is particularly brilliant, don't you think?"

"Majesty, there are some things for which there can only be one answer, not two or three.

"Only one answer? Only one? Wilson!" His face became infused with red streaks as his temper rose. "You are an intolerant bigot! There is no place for closed-minded people in my kingdom. You will be punished for that opinion, I can assure you."

"Yes, your majesty. I am sure I will be." In a softer voice he added, "Even though some things cannot be changed with a royal decree." He brightened. "Right now I think we had best get you to safety. I see that the fire is spreading and that the wind is blowing it toward the palace."

The acrid tang of smoke began to permeate the throne room as Mr. Wilson hurried the king out a side door.

Think on These Things

1. The story contains two examples, brought by the baker and the sergeant, of ways in which allowing a number to stand for both its numerical value and the number of letters the number word contains can create problems. What are those two examples? What is the numerical difference between the amount indicated by using the numerical value and using the letter value?

2. What would happen if the price of a potato was usually three coppers, yet the grocer insisted on receiving six coppers under the king's new plan? How would the grocer justify this new price? How do you think the king would rule if a housewife who was buying potatoes from the grocer brought her case to the king's court because of a dispute over the price of potatoes?

3. Can you think of other examples in which allowing the king's progressive ideas about numbers would cause difficulties and questions? Write two or three brief scenarios that would provide additional illustrations of ways in which the king's ideas would need further explanation or clarification.

4. In "New Math," the king's ideas caused a real problem when the armory exploded and the city appeared to be catching on fire. The Rulebook calls for 1.5 scoops of gunpowder in the cannon, yet the captain put in seven scoops. Is the story realistic in this scenario?

What do you imagine would happen if seven scoops of gunpowder were put in a cannon designed for 1.5 scoops?

5. Do you think that the king's new way of using numbers is a good one? Why or why not? What do you think will happen to the baker's business if the king's new decree continues? Project what might happen to the kingdom in the future if the king continues to insist that his new decree be followed.

6. What motivation does the story suggest the king has for accepting the professors' ideas for this new way of using mathematics? While the story may be a bit far-fetched, is this motivation one that you see operating in the world today? Give three current examples of ways in which people desire to be progressive and open to new ideas. Are there some examples you can think of in which this motivation leads to less than desirable conclusions?

7. In the story, numbers are allowed to have more than one interpreted meaning. For example, "two" can mean 2 or 3, and "three" can mean 3 or 5. Are there some things in real life that are like numbers and should have only one interpretation? This is a difficult question to think about, but an important one. Are there some things that are true, no matter what? What are those things? What happens when people try to give more than one meaning to something that really has only one meaning?

Angels Watching Over Me

"How beautiful!" exclaimed Mother as she helped young Jimmy out of the car. The church parking lot was covered with a thin dusting of sparkling white snow, as the stars pierced the black canopy of the sky with their white-blue fire.

Father was getting little Hannah out of her car seat and paused to look around. There were several cars in the parking lot already. He could hear the faint notes of the piano coming from inside the church, playing "It Came Upon a Midnight Clear." The windows were a warm, buttery yellow, lit by the candles inside. He, too, looked up into the vast sky and drew in a deep, stirring breath of the cold, crisp air. "Yes, my dear," said Father. "A perfectly beautiful night."

The little family's feet crunched across the snow as they approached the sanctuary, Father carrying Hannah in his arms, Jimmy's hand in Mother's.

One of the deacons opened the door for them and they were bathed in the warmth inside – a warmth that was not only physical, but spiritual, emanating from the quietly reverent saints already sitting in the pews, bathed in candle light and the sweet sounds of the Christmas hymn played on the piano. The deacon's wife smiled as she hugged Mother.

"Isn't it beautiful?" she whispered. "So peaceful!"

Father, Mother, Jimmy and Hannah slid into a pew near the back. One by one, families were coming forward to be served Communion by the pastor. Jimmy watched as the pastor quietly met each family, serving them the bread and the wine. He knew what those things meant – Father had explained to him about how the baby Jesus had grown up to be a Man, and how he had given up his life for others. And how He really was God, come down to Earth. Jimmy didn't understand it all, but he knew that the bread represented Jesus' body, and that the wine represented His blood. More than anything, Jimmy knew that Jesus had made a great sacrifice so that everyone – Father, Mother, Hannah, and even Jimmy – might be able to be with God. Mother reached over and squeezed Jimmy's hand. He noticed there were bright tears in Mother's eyes that reflected the candlelight. He had heard about tears of joy. He had a lump in his own throat, too.

One by one, the families came forward to receive the Lord's Supper. One by one, the pastor quietly spoke of Jesus' gift to the world. One by one, he prayed with them. Jimmy watched as the pastor's son and daughter-in-law whispered in the pastor's ear. It must have been something that made the pastor very happy, for he smiled and hugged them both close to him. There were even tears in the pastor's eyes.

Jimmy watched as Joe and Miss Shirley came forward, holding hands. The pastor raised his hands in praise at the sight and hugged them. Jimmy watched as old Mr. Gabbard came forward. Mr. Gabbard was by himself, but the pastor spent a lot of time talking quietly with him before serving Mr. Gabbard the bread and the wine.

When it was their turn, Father and Mother, Jimmy and Hannah went forward. They sat in the pew as the pastor gave Father and Mother the bread. Jimmy knew that Hannah was too little, but he received his little bit of bread from the pastor, who said, "Jimmy, this is the body of Christ. Now that you have accepted Christ as your savior, He welcomes you to His table." Jimmy wasn't sure he knew what that meant, but he knew that he now belonged to God. He was grateful to Jesus for being willing to give up His life. He looked up at Father and Mother, who were looking down at him, smiling, holding their bit of bread in their hands. Together, they took Communion.

They did the same with the wine that the pastor brought to them. Jimmy squirmed around to look and see who else had come into the church, but Mother patted his arm so he sat, quietly listening to the beautiful music and letting the candlelight and the sharp Christmassy smell of the freshly cut pine branches wash over him. He sat, quiet and still, with his father and mother and his little sister in their little church on Christmas Eve.

The pastor invited them to join him, and Jimmy put his little hand in the pastor's big one as they stood in a circle. The pastor prayed a beautiful prayer – Jimmy couldn't remember everything the pastor said, but he remembered that the pastor prayed for blessings on them, and that the coming year would be a time of knowing God even better. "Yes," thought Jimmy. "That's what I want, too."

Mother hugged the pastor and Jimmy heard her whisper "Congratulations!" in his ear. Father shook the pastor's hand, and Jimmy did too. Little Hannah, who had fallen asleep in Father's arm, received a kiss.

Then they quietly left the warm glow of the sanctuary for the brisk cold of the out of doors. The shock made Jimmy take deep lungs-full of the cold air, watching his breath steam from his mouth and nostrils as he exhaled.

Mother's eyes were still moist. "That," she said, her voice catching a tiny bit, "Was wonderful. What a blessing on Christmas Eve."

"Every time we have Communion, I'm struck again by the miracle of it all," said Father. "God sending his Son to be born in a manger. Jesus being willing to pay the penalty for my sin, and giving us the Lord's Supper to remind us. What a miracle!"

Jimmy looked up into the night sky and saw the stars, and something else, beside.

"What a miracle," echoed Mother. "And what a sense of peace in the sanctuary. It was as if everything that was wrong has been made right."

"They don't call it a sanctuary for nothing. Did you see any miracles tonight, Jimmy?" Father asked quietly.

Jimmy was still staring upward, trying to make out just what it was he was seeing.

"I believe I did," said Mother.

"How so?" asked Father.

"I believe the pastor is going to be a grandfather."

"Ah!" Father laughed. "Is that what that meant? You're always two steps ahead of me. Did you notice that, Jimmy?"

Jimmy was barely hearing them. Whatever it was that he was seeing was coming into focus. Something shimmery and light was arching up over the steeple of the church and coming down around the parking lot.

"It sure was good to see Joe and Shirley together tonight."

"Wasn't it though?" said Mother. "I hope this means they've worked out their differences. They've been separated for far too long."

"Another miracle?" said Father. "And did you see Mr. Gabbard? Unless I miss my guess, another soul was added to the Lord's flock tonight."

"Praise God!" said Mother. "I've been praying for Mr. Gabbard for so long now. That's a real miracle, if there ever was one." She looked down at Jimmy who was intently gazing upward. "Jimmy, you've gone all quiet. Did you see any miracles tonight?"

Jimmy didn't answer, but only pointed up to the miracle that was just becoming visible to him. Father and Mother saw them, too. There were four of them, one standing at each corner of the parking lot, guarding the church. They were certainly Angels, although not angels like Jimmy had ever imagined. There were not sweet little babies that looked like Hannah when she just had a diaper on. No, these were tall and powerful Beings, clothed in light that you could see through, but that were very real none the less. Each Angel had a sword and the sword was drawn, held out in front to ward off any attack or evil that might come against the church.

Mother made a sharp intake of breath. "Oh my ..." Her words were lost in wonder.

"No wonder there is such a feeling of peace here. With guardians like that ..." Father had no words to describe what he was seeing.

The vision began to fade, starting at the ground. The Angel's feet began to disappear, then their shimmery robes. Jimmy looked up and up, into the top of the night sky, and saw their enormous wings, soaring up over the church, guarding and protecting it, almost touching way up over the steeple.

"Father," asked Jimmy as the tips of the wings disappeared, "Are the Angels still there, even though we can't see them?"

"I believe so, son. We've been privileged to catch a tiny glimpse of them, but I believe they are there at every moment, guarding us, guarding our church."

"Father, is that a miracle?"

"Yes, indeed, son," said Father quietly. "One of many miracles tonight. One of many."

Think on These Things

1. Write your own definition of miracle. What makes something a miracle?

2. Do you believe in miracles? Have you ever seen a miracle, or has a miracle ever happened to you?

3. "Angels Watching Over Me" is a story about miracles. How would you react if you saw four angels like Jimmy saw? Would you believe your eyes or would you think it was an illusion or a hallucination?

4. The story has other elements, besides Jimmy's vision of the four angels, that are described as miracles. What are those things? Do you agree or disagree that these events are miracles? Give reasons for your opinion.

5. Given your definition of miracle in question 1, and your response to question 4, go back and revisit question 2. Are there miracles that you have witnessed or been a part of?

6. "Angels Watching Over Me" implies that there are angels guarding the church on Christmas Eve. Do you believe in angels? If so, what role, if any, do you think they have in your life? What do you think an angel might look like? Where did you get your ideas about the appearance of angels? Have you ever seen an angel?

7. The story centers on a communion service at a church. What do you know about a communion service? Do some research on communion and its meaning, either for your own, or for other Christian faith traditions.

Every Jew a Wanted Jew

"I made the request for our Jew last night." Müeller said it matter-of-factly as he opened with queen's pawn to queen four.

It was a crisp, clear autumn day. Cold enough to wear a coat, but not so cold as to be anything other than invigorating. Müeller pulled his coat around him a bit and waited for Schmidt's response. Müeller always opened with his queen's pawn, if he was playing white. And Schmidt almost always responded with his queen's pawn as well. Müeller stared at the board, willing Schmidt to make his move.

Schmidt made no effort to move a piece. Instead he said, "You requested that Goldstein be ... sent away?"

"Yes, he really was becoming quite burdensome, you know. Go ahead and move the pawn, Schmidt. You know you will."

The air smelled wonderful. The leaves were mostly down from the trees, now, and skittered before the small breeze like tiny animals prancing across the pavement. The park was not particularly crowded. Müeller and Schmidt were the only two playing chess today, but a couple of teenagers were kicking around a football.

Schmidt also looked at the board, but still did not select a piece. His hand did not even hover over the board, as Müeller expected when Schmidt was close to making up his mind.

"You had him sent away, just like that?"

"Yes, yes. Of course. I had him sent to the Centre, as is my legal right. As I said, he was becoming quite a nuisance."

Schmidt didn't reply, although there was a look on his face that Müeller couldn't quite decipher. Either Schmidt was suddenly stumped by a simple opening move in chess, or something was bothering him. Müeller usually won when they played together, but that didn't mean that Schmidt was a poor player. Far from it; he gave Müeller a good game almost every time they played. Usually they met in the park on Tuesdays for two or three games. It was a pleasant way to spend the time, especially when the weather was fine.

Schmidt finally moved his queen's pawn, as Müeller had fully expected he would. Müeller responded promptly by moving out his bishop. Of course Schmidt wouldn't fall for the fool's mate gambit, but it was a solid opening anyway. Next he'd work on shoring up his pawn defenses, and then bring out his favorites, the knights.

Schmidt studied the board again, then moved his king's knight.

"A departure from your usual strategy, Schmidt!" Müeller was delighted. Perhaps this would be a more challenging game. "Well done."

Schmidt sighed. "I feel that something must change." He observed as Müeller moved his other bishop. "You really had Goldstein ... ?" The question hovered in the air over the board.

"Yes, I said." Müeler's tone betrayed his impatience. "Why this sudden interest in the Jew we had at our house? Can we not just play chess?"

"I suppose. But it just seems so ... so final. I guess I just can't quite believe it. Had Goldstein done anything in particular?"

"No, nothing like that. As Jews go, he was just fine. Didn't get in the way much, wasn't particularly obnoxious or that sort of thing. Really, nothing serious to complain about. The wife rather liked him. But we just decided that we'd had him long enough. The time had come to send him away. It was just a choice we made." Schmidt moved another piece and Müeller quickly responded. They played several more moves in silence, exchanging a few pieces in minor skirmishes.

"You didn't want him any more?"

Back to that again. "Not really. I believe every Jew should be a wanted Jew, don't you? I mean, it just isn't fair to them to have them living in conditions where they aren't wanted, is it? We just didn't want ours any more."

"I see." Schmidt made an unusual move with his rook that caught Müeller off guard. Müeller had to think for a few moments. He realized he was forced to castle defensively.

Schmidt's mind wandered to the Jews living at his house. There were four, now, and rumors of a fifth that would come soon. His wife had a bit of a time of it, stretching the grocery budget to feed that crowd. But they were happy. Everyone worked, pulling their fair share, helping each other. In the evenings they sang songs and one of the Jews played the squeezebox. A bit crowded, perhaps, but not something they couldn't manage.

Perhaps he should send the new fellow away that was rumored to arrive soon. Or, once he arrived, perhaps he should turn him in. One less mouth to feed.

Of course it was his legal right. Everyone knew that. And, as Müeller had put it so well, every Jew should be wanted. If you didn't want them, it wasn't fair to keep them around in an unwanted condition. That just made sense.

But still, there was something about it that all seemed so ... so cold-hearted.

"Schmidt!" Müeller could tell that Schmidt was distracted by something, the way he sat with his chin in his hand staring at the board. "Schmidt! It's your move." Müeller looked at him; Schmidt wasn't really looking at the board for his eyes were unfocused, thinking about something. Almost absentmindedly, Schmidt reached out and moved his queen. Again, it was a surprisingly bold move for Schmidt. Müeller smiled to himself. A good game in the making – but he saw a weakness on Schmidt's left flank. He moved his knight in, coming close to threatening Schmidt's king. He could see it in his mind's eye – the careful arrangement of pieces he was beginning to build, some threatening Schmidt's king, others in supporting roles. He would have to sacrifice his rook, of course, and probably the queen. But victory was no more than eight moves away, possibly as few as six if Schmidt did not wake up to the danger quickly enough.

"I don't know. It all seems somewhat callous, rather inhumane. To have Goldstein put away just because he was, well, inconvenient." He moved his rook to block one of Müeller's plans. Good, thought Müeller to himself, a good game. Still, victory in eight, unless he was missing something.

He pressed his advantage. "Check," he said, and smiled.

Schmidt studied the board a long time before moving his king.

"It isn't inhumane at all," said Müeller. "Quite the reverse. What is inhumane is keeping a Jew that is no longer wanted. We did the fellow a favor."

"Did he go willingly? Did he struggle?"

"I really couldn't say. I simply called the authorities and they took him away. Schmidt, it really is of no significance. He was no longer wanted. He was sent away to be terminated, perfectly within the letter and intent of the law."

"Yes, but is the law right?" Schmidt looked directly at Müeller as he made his next move. "It may be legal, but is it right?"

"Of course, of course." Müeller made his next move impatiently, tightening the noose further on Schmidt's king. "We should have a choice, should we not? After all, we live in a free society, do we not? I should have the choice, the right to decide, whether or not to keep my Jews."

"What if the Jew in question has a different opinion?"

Müeller laughed. "What a foolish notion, Schmidt. Their opinions are of no consequence. You really should pay more attention to the game." He moved another piece. "Check."

"I can understand the notion of these decisions being made on the basis of guilt or innocence. I may not agree with it, but at least the idea is defensible. But to send a Jew for termination simply because ... " His voice trailed off. "I like Goldstein. He is – was – a nice chap." He decisively moved his rook down the side of the board where it was suddenly threatening several of Müeller's back ranks and coming surprisingly close to his king.

"Look, Schmidt. Let us not discuss it further. You know that I have the right to make my own choice about my own Jew, just as I support your right to make your own choices. The law clearly supports my right to do so. And, it is the compassionate thing to do. As I said, every Jew should be a wanted Jew. I can't imagine anything more miserable than being a Jew, and an unwanted Jew at that." He shivered a bit as the afternoon shadows lengthened and the wind picked up.

They both looked up at the clatter of wheels being driven along the cobblestones beside the park. It was a scraping, hollow noise. It was the familiar wagon, no writing on the sides, but familiar none the less. It was the wagon that transported Jews to the Centre. Müeller only glanced. He'd seen the wagon before, knew perfectly well what it was, didn't give it another thought. Just another part of life in this city.

But Schmidt looked more intently. For some reason the conversation today had made him uneasy. He followed the wagon's slow, noisy track down the road beside the park. As the wagon drew opposite the chess board, Schmidt could see a pair of hands gripping the bars in the back. As the wagon drew past, he could see, first a nose, then the rest of a face, pressed against the bars. He saw the small, terrified eyes. He recognized the face. It was Müeller's Jew; it was Goldstein. Impulsively Schmidt got to his feet as he heard Müeller's vague protest. Schmidt's eyes met Goldstein's, their gazes locked on each other for moments as the wagon drew past. Schmidt reached for his cap and took it off, clutching it to his chest. Goldstein's eyes pierced into Schmidt's. Neither man spoke. The wagon pulled away and was lost from view.

"Come! Come!" said Müeller impatiently. "The game. Let's return to the game."

"I suppose you are right. All the same ... "

Schmidt's next move was completely unexpected – Müeller had not seen it coming. Using an insignificant pawn as the key, Schmidt had constructed an inescapable trap, which he now sprung on Müeller's unprotected king.

"Checkmate," said Schmidt.

Think on These Things

1. Without analyzing your feelings too much, what one word would you use to describe your reaction to this story? Now think about your reaction a bit more deeply. Why did you react this way? What was it about the subject matter that made you feel as you do?

2. The setting of this story is unspecified. Yet the names of the two main characters and the topic of conversation evoke a certain place and time. What is that place and time? Do you think the choice of setting by the author is deliberate? Why or why not?

3. Construct the legal ramifications of the conversation between the two men. What is the relationship between men like Müeller and Schmidt, and the Jewish people living amongst them? What are the legal rights of men like Müeller and Schmidt relative to Jews? According to the story, what are the legal rights of Jewish people in the society in which they live?

4. The story constructs a legal system that has some similarities to Germany in the early 1940s. But there are some definite differences, too. Research the legal status of Jews under the Third Reich and compare that status to the status of Jews in this story. What are the similarities? What are the differences?

5. Contrast the beliefs and attitudes of the two main characters in the story, particularly in their relationship to Jewish people. First look at Müeller. What are Müeller's attitudes toward Jews? Would you characterize his attitude towards Jews as being compassionate? Why or why not?

6. Now focus on Schmidt. What are Schmidt's attitudes toward Jews? Do you think he has conflicting notions about Jewish people? Why or why not? When the wagon pulls past the chess game, Schmidt stands up. Why do you think he does that? What thoughts do you think are going through his mind?

7. Which of the two men, Müeller or Schmidt, appeal to you most? What do you like about the men, and why? What do you dislike, and why?

8. If you could write the story a different way, how would you have it end? Would you have Müeller or Schmidt do something differently? Write an outline of a different ending.

9. Do your friends and acquaintances demonstrate attitudes that reflect the attitudes of Müeller and Schmidt? In what ways? In the larger community in which you live, do you find any attitudes similar to those seen in Müeller and Schmidt? Give examples.

10. In the story, Jews appeared to have few legal rights, if any. In any society, what is the source of the legal rights of people who live in

that society? In the story, would you say that
Jews were treated like people, or like
something else (and, if so, what else)? What
happens to legal rights when a group is not
treated as if they are people? What happens
to a society when this happens?

Light on Berea's Ridge

John Rogers reined in his horse. "Whoah, Barnabas. Let's stop a minute." He looked out over the Glade. Rogers' ride from Richmond had been long, and he was anxious to be home. But he paused for a moment to give thanks for the opportunity he had for serving here in the little community known as Berea.

The sun was sinking toward the west, casting a golden light on the ridge opposite him. Up there, unseen in the thick growth, was the fledgling school where Rogers, his wife Elizabeth, Reverend Fee and the others taught and ministered. He could just make out a wisp of chimney smoke rising above the tall oaks and maples. The ridge curved around the Glade, creating what Rogers had laughingly, in a moment of academic jocularity, dubbed the "ellipse." Now, from his vantage point upon his horse, it seemed to Rogers that the light of Providence was bathing the Berea ridge with blessing. "It is quite a sight, Barnabas, is it not?" Rogers asked his horse. He flicked the reins and his mount began to thread its way across the Glade and up toward the ridge.

Not that living on the Berea ridge was easy. Living in Kentucky in the 1850s was rough. He and Elizabeth had built their home out of logs, even as she had tended to the needs of the students and of their own new baby, and even as he had gone about teaching and gaining support for the Berea school. Much of their day was spent on what could only be thought of as subsistence; raising food, chopping wood, providing shelter. But he and Elizabeth went about the work with enthusiasm because working at Berea was, for them, a life's calling.

Physical hardships were mild compared to the spiritual battles they fought. Ignorance of Scripture was one obstacle. Reverend Fee had named the little school Berea in the hopes that people here would be "of more noble character," just as they had been in Saint Paul's day of old when they would "search the Scriptures daily" to see if the things Paul said were true. Rogers and Reverend Fee actively encouraged their students to look to the Bible for truth and to act upon the wisdom they found there.

One such truth was found in Acts 17:26, "God hath made of one blood all nations of men." Rogers and Fee and others knew this to mean that all people, regardless of the color of their skin, regardless of social standing, were God's creation and, as such, entitled to learn of Jesus Christ. Thus their school did not shy away from the controversy of declaring that both Negroes and whites were welcome at Berea. In fact, the school's constitution declared that anyone of "good moral character" was welcome.

The path opened up into a clearing flooded with yellow afternoon sunlight. A man with skin the color of ripe polk berries was chopping weeds in a small garden patch. "Afternoon, Sam!" Rogers sang out.

"Hullo, Reveren' Rogers," Sam replied. "Where you been?"

"Up to Richmond to visit some folks who may send their children to the school," replied Rogers. "How have things been, here?"

"Bout the same." Sam propped one threadbare elbow on his hoe handle. "It shore is good to have a bit to eat, a place to sleep, an' to know Jesus, ain't it?"

"It is, indeed, Sam."

"It shore is good to be free, too." There was a twinkle in the man's eye.

"It is Christ who makes us free, Sam."

"Yassah, thas' true. Yes indeed." Sam went back to his chopping. "God bless you, Reveren' Rogers. Watch out for the storm."

"God bless you, Sam." Rogers noted the looming thunderheads out to the west. "I'll be careful."

The trail narrowed again and became steeper as he drew closer to the ridge. He heard, before he saw, the horse and rider coming down the trail toward him. As he rounded a bend, he saw that it was Zeb Ray Jones from Rockcastle, a slaveholder rumored to be a member of the night riders. Rogers' jaw tightened as he encountered a man toward whom he struggled to feel charitable.

"Mr. Jones." Rogers tipped his hat.

"Reverend Rogers." Jones eased his mount to one side of the trail to let Rogers pass. "Beautiful day, isn't it?"

"Beautiful, indeed." Even as he said it, the first shadows from the clouds of the pending storm began dimming the light on the trail.

What would Zeb Ray Jones be doing on the Berea ridge, Rogers wondered to himself as he continued up the trail. A man like Zeb Ray Jones would ordinarily not have received a particularly warm welcome on the ridge, not because of who he was, but because of what he did. Rogers and Fee had both been adamant that slaveholding was a wrong practice. Many times both men had searched the Scriptures and had always come away with the same conclusion: the practice of one man owning another as his property was wrong. The law may condone it, popular opinion may support it, but the small community at Berea were against it. The storms of war were undoubtedly brewing in the north and south, but, here on the Berea ridge, the fledgling school "walked worthy of its calling" by welcoming both Negroes and whites. So why would a known slaveholder like Zeb Ray Jones be visiting at Berea? Rogers drew his cloak around him as the storm clouds occluded the sun, turning the bright path into a dim, gloomy trail.

As Barnabas neared the clearing, the horse sensed that home and provender were near. Rogers gave him free reign to canter toward the barn. Observing the clearing with its church, school and small cluster of log homes, Rogers didn't see anything amiss. But thoughts of Zeb Ray Jones continued to haunt him. He took the saddle off of Barnabas and put it away, rubbing down his trusted friend and giving him a measure of feed. Then he turned his own feet toward home.

Elizabeth, their young son on her hip, greeted him at the door. "My dear," he said, kissing her on the cheek, "You grow lovelier every time I see you!"

"John! How you talk! Say hello to Papa, son."

John scooped up the little boy and held him high in the air. "Have you been a good boy for your mother?"

The child giggled with delight and, to the young parent's ears, made sounds that certainly meant "mommy" and "daddy."

Rogers drew his wife to him and encircled her and their son with his arms. "Has anything happened today, my dear? I saw Zeb Ray Jones on the trail and it caused me some alarm."

"Zeb Ray Jones! Did he say anything? Did he threaten you, John?"

"No, nothing like that, my dear. He was actually quite pleasant. I just don't know what to make of him being here on the ridge. Perhaps I'd better go have a word with Reverend Fee." He kissed Elizabeth again and left, caught off guard, as he had been so many times before, by the blessings God had provided him in this sturdy and beautiful helpmate.

He crossed the clearing toward the Fee home and knocked on the door. Mrs. Fee let him in and showed him to the study where Reverend Fee was working at his desk. "Well, good evening John," said Fee, rising and shaking his hand warmly. "Back from Richmond I see. Have a profitable journey?"

"I think so. Mr. Parks will, most likely, send his two sons here to school next fall. Reverend Andrews will send three daughters and his oldest boy."

"Good! Good. Have a seat, John. I'm glad you've come."

Rogers sat in the indicated chair as Fee settled himself back at his desk. "I saw Zeb Ray Jones on the trail coming down off of the ridge as I was returning to Berea just now," said Rogers.

"Indeed," said Fee. "I just met with Mr. Jones not an hour ago."

"You did! What would Mr. Jones want with us here?"

"He wants to send his children here to school. He knows of our high academic standards, due, in no small part, to your and Mrs. Rogers' work. He had hoped to gain their admission to the school."

"You told him no, of course."

"I did not. Mr. Jones is a wealthy man, capable of providing our school with needed capital. He also recognizes our academic strength. I could not turn him away."

"But he is a slaveholder! Zeb Ray Jones engages in a practice abhorrent to everything we hold dear!"

"Is he not, John, a creature of God? Hath not God created of one blood all peoples of the earth?"

"Of course he is, Reverend Fee. The Bible says 'God hath created of one blood all nations of men.' It says that in Christ, there is neither male nor female, Greek nor Jew, bond nor free. But we cannot condone the practice of owning slaves!" Rogers stood up and paced to the window.

"Now, John, calm yourself! We are not necessarily condoning slaveholding just because we admit the children of a slave owner to this school."

"But Reverend Fee, may I remind you of our constitution? Admission to Berea is open to all who are of 'good moral character.' We have all sinned and have fallen short of the glory of God. But are we now saying that owning slaves is acceptable behavior? Are we to redefine morality because it is pragmatic to do so, because of popular pressure or because of money?"

"Take care, Reverend Rogers, in what you imply. Admitting Zeb Ray Jones' children is not being done because of financial considerations— although I admit to you that Mr. Jones' financial resources will be welcome to our treasury. Think, instead, sir, of the children. Do they not deserve an education?"

"Of course, of course. However, there are other options open to a man of Mr. Jones' resources. My deep concern is that admitting the Jones children compromises our mission here; it turns a blind eye toward an abhorrent practice and, by default, supports it. We cannot do this thing!"

"On the contrary, John. It is the right thing to do. God has made of one blood all peoples of the earth. Christ welcomes all."

"Yes, yes, that is absolutely true. You persist in quoting that phrase. But there is more to it." He gazed out the window at the gathering gloom. The storm was now almost upon them and the light that had earlier shown golden on the ridge was now all but choked off. He turned back to Fee. "Christ welcomes all to the gift of His salvation. But Christ does not welcome all behavior. Did He not drive the moneychangers out of the temple? Did He not require the rich young ruler to give away all that he had if he was to follow Him? Zeb Ray Jones engages in an evil practice. Does God's Word not instruct us have no fellowship with sin? Did you, yourself, Reverend Fee, not instruct the congregations of more than one church to expel and have no fellowship slave holders?"

"I was young, when I said those things, and inexperienced."

"No! You were right! Berea must take a strong stand against slavery. Admitting the Jones children will send a strong message—the wrong message—that slavery is acceptable. I rely only on God's word for instruction and His Word is clear on this point."

"But the children, John. Think of the children."

"If your concern for the children was genuine, you would also be concerned for the children of Mr. Jones' slaves. But I have heard no mention of them. I am astonished, Reverend Fee, in your thinking about this. It seems, at best, inconsistent and misguided." Fee was silhouetted in the window opposite. Rogers could not make out the expression on his face, only the outline of his head as Fee sat at his desk. To Rogers, he appeared to be speaking from the shadows.

"There, there, John. You simply have yet to be enlightened about this matter. It will come to you in time, I have no doubt." He turned back to his desk. "Mr. Jones' children will be admitted to school in the fall."

"I must protest, Reverend Fee. Doing so is wrong! It will, in the end, imperil our work here on this ridge."

"Never the less. Good day, Reverend Rogers."

"Good day." Rogers let himself out, pulling his cloak around him as the wind of the coming storm came down through the oaks and maples. Head down, he trudged back to his own cabin, where Elizabeth had prepared the evening meal.

They held hands as Rogers offered the blessing for their meager meal and ate, mostly in silence. After they had washed up and put away the dishes, Rogers sat reading his Bible by lantern light. "Lord," he prayed, "make me of more noble character. Teach me what You have to say. My heart longs to know You and Your teachings, and none other." Time passed. There were no new revelations, no shadow of changing, only confirmation of truths that were already in evidence and that had been for time immemorial.

Elizabeth Rogers came and put her arms around her husband. "Time for bed, my love." She kissed his head as he sat in the chair, Bible on his lap.

"Yes, my dear." He rubbed his eyes and laid the Bible carefully on the shelf. "Coming," he said.

With a heavy heart, John Rogers got ready for bed and lay down next to his wife. She cuddled beside him, her nearness giving him comfort in the midst of his concern. He could not sleep, but lay watching the one candle on the bed stand flicker, flicker, getting weaker. Finally it went completely out. The room, and the Berea ridge, were cloaked in darkness.

Think on These Things

1. While this story is a complete work of fiction, the characters of Reverend John R. R. Rogers, his wife Elizabeth, and Reverend John G. Fee are real. So is the school that was started in Berea, Kentucky in 1855. What can you find out about the school that these men started? What was its purpose?

2. Continue your research and find out what happened to these men and their school in the years leading up to the Civil War and the years that immediately followed? What did these men believe was their purpose? Who wanted to thwart their purpose? What were the results?

3. Imagine living in the Appalachian Mountains in Kentucky in the mid 1800s. What would life have been like? Would you consider it to have been a hard life? In view of living conditions that families like the Fees and the Rogers endured, how remarkable do you think it is that they found and pursued a larger purpose that resulted in a school that survives to this day? Why is that?

4. In the story, the fictional Rev. John G. Fee takes a stand that is inconsistent with the stand he took in real life. What are the differences between the fictional Fee and the historical Fee? How do you think the historical Fee would have responded to the fictional Fee's decision to allow Zeb Ray Jones' children admission to the school?

Would he have approved? Had the fictional Fee's attitude been the historical Fee's approach, what kind of school would Berea be today, or would it even have existed? Why or why not?

5. Discuss the importance of principles in life. The historical Fee and Rogers were men of strong conviction, immense integrity, and unwavering principles. How important are these attributes today? What happens when principles are undermined or left untended?

6. As the title, "Light on Berea's Ridge" implies, light plays an important role in this story. List the places where light is mentioned in the story. How is light used as an allegory in the story? It the use effective or not? Discuss your reasons.

7. Do some Biblical research. Find the places in the story in which Scripture is quoted or the quotation is implied. Particularly note the conversation between Fee and Rogers in Fee's cabin. Compare the quotation that both Fee and Rogers make of Acts 17:26. How are they different? While the answer lies in an anachronism, why do you think the different quotations were used in this story?

8. What can you find out about Berea today? Why was the school at Berea so named? To what degree do you think the school today follows, or not follow, the original purposes set forth by Rev. John G. Fee, Rev. J. R. R Rogers and others? Defend your opinion.

A Good Place

"Daddy?" The young girl's voice had the tiniest edge of fear in it. "Daddy, are you out here?" She swung her flashlight in an arc, illuminating small circles of the yard and the woods. There was no moon. And it was cold. She could see her breath when the flashlight beam intersected with her exhaled exertions. She flashed the light around the yard, searching, afraid of what she might find. Or not find.

Her feet crunched as she walked across the yard. A light snow had fallen during the day, and after sunset the temperature had dropped well below freezing so that the snow was now a thin coating of ice crystals. Each step made a sharp, squeaky sound. She flashed the beam back over her path. Each step was clearly outlined, like dark puddles against the white background of the snow. *What was that?* Her heart raced until she recognized the cat following her.

"Kitty, kitty," she cried, almost too loudly, bravely calling into the night air. "Here, kitty kitty." The cat continued its leisurely pace, using the girl's footprints to keep its paws dry.

When the cat reached her, the girl bent down and scratched its ears. "Hello, Harper, I'm glad you're here." The cat purred, as she always did for her favorite mistress. "Let's go find Daddy. Mommy says she thinks he's out in the barn." She stood, turned, and bravely resumed her trek toward the gate in the fence.

Now that she had the company of the cat, she was able to look around her a bit more. While the woods were still dark and impenetrable to the beam of her flashlight, she did note the stars. It was a very clear night, so that the stars seemed like intense pin-pricks of the brightest fire imaginable.

"Daddy?" she called again.

She found the chain on the gate more by feel than by sight. The metal burned her bare hands, it was so cold. *I wish I thought to put on gloves.* A gust of wind made the pine trees to the west whistle in a mournful way. She closed the gate and trudged on. Now the grass was thicker, where the animals hadn't cropped it so closely, and it was rougher going. The crust of snow was no longer smooth, but bumpy, hiding tufts of grass that clung to her boots, forcing her to pick up her feet higher to step over them.

As she crested the hill, she saw the lights of Mr. Austin's house. Christmas lights dangled from each eave and gutter. Reindeer, outlined in lights, performed a mechanical ballet, moving their heads up and down and their antlers side to side. A plastic Santa and sleigh gave the impression it was taking off from the rooftop. The sudden brightness of the lights briefly blinded the girl, until her eyes adjusted and she turned to focus on the barn.

She flashed her light around the doors of the small structure, catching glimpses of several animals inside. The light aroused their interest and two goats poked their head out of the door, sounding a quiet and inquisitive "Mmmbaah?" at her. Their eyes glowed a pale green in the light.

"Hello goats," she said. Then, more loudly, "Daddy, are you in there?"

"Yes, Susan, I'm in here with the goats." The deep and familiar voice of her father sounded quietly out of the depths of the doorway.

Susan stepped up to the doorway and flashed the light around, blinding her father as she did so. He put up his hand to shield his eyes and she quickly moved the light, but not before she had seen that he was sitting on a hay bale, leaned back against the rough planks of the barn wall, with the goats around him. He had one arm draped against the feed trough as he blocked the beam of her flashlight with the other. The goats were mostly lying down, quietly chewing their cud with their familiar rhythmic chomp, chomp, chomp. Their jaws moved side to side as they peacefully completed the second half of a ruminant's business of eating. A few goats were standing and now nosed her jeans and pockets inquisitively. Instinctively she pulled her coat away from one that thought she might try a taste of the hem.

"What are you doing in here, Daddy?"

"Just sitting here, honey. Come here and sit beside me." He made room on the hay bale and she sat down.

He put his arm around her and she snuggled close, his warmth and the familiar smell of his Bay Rum aftershave mingling with the earthy smells of hay, manure and goat musk. Suddenly she found herself exhaling into the cold air, releasing the tension of her trek through the snow and darkness. She snuggled closer.

The cat, Harper, threaded her aloof path between the reclining goats and poured her furry form through a crack between two boards in the barn wall.

"Why don't you turn out the flashlight, honey?"

"But Daddy, it's dark!" But she turned out the light anyway.

They sat in relative silence, listening to the chewing of the goats, the wind in the pines around the barn, the thousand sounds that fill a winter night if you stop and listen.

"Mommy said you were in the barn, Daddy. What are you doing out here?"

"Well, Susan." He snuggled her even closer. "I like to come out to the barn on Christmas Eve because it reminds me of the night Jesus was born."

"Oh! You mean He was born in a stable?"

"That's right. It may not have looked like our goat barn, but I imagine it wasn't a very fine place. It probably had animals in it – sheep and donkeys, perhaps. And there was certainly a manger."

"What's a manger, Daddy?"

"This." He patted the feed trough. "Baby Jesus' mother and father used a feed trough – a manger – as His first bed."

"Mary and Joseph." She nodded, wisely. "Because there was no room for them in the inn."

"Good girl! That's exactly right. I'm sure Mary would have rather had her baby in a nice warm bed, but there just wasn't any room, and they had to come out to a stable to have the baby. A stable that might be a lot like this one." He paused and they absorbed the quiet together. "And they laid Him in a manger."

"Baby Jesus grew up to be a King, didn't He, Daddy?"

"Yes, honey, He did. The King of Kings and the Lord of Lords."

"But it doesn't seem like a king should be born in a barn."

"No, it sure doesn't. A barn is dark, and dirty. Maybe it even smells bad. It doesn't seem like a fitting place for a king to be born, does it? And yet Baby Jesus was willing to be born in a place like this."

Susan pondered this a while. "Daddy, why do you think that is?"

"Well, Susan, I'm glad you asked. I think I know, and it is the reason I like to come out to the barn on Christmas Eve and think about His birth so long ago."

She waited.

"The reason is that I think our lives are a lot like this barn. A little messy. A little dirty. Sometimes our lives even smell bad. Sometimes they are very dark"

"I'm going to take a bath before I go to bed tonight." It was said matter-of-factly.

Her father chuckled and hugged her. "I know you are. After all, tomorrow is Christmas!

"But I'm not talking about the kind of dirt that will wash off in a bathtub. I'm talking about a kind of dirt that makes our lives displeasing to God. He wants us to be good and kind and helpful – and so often we disappoint Him."

"You mean like the time I punched Jeffie in the stomach because he spilled his milk on me?"

"Yes, like that. Or when you tell mommy you have brushed your teeth and you really haven't. Or when you grab one of Jeffie's toys and won't play with him."

"Oh, Daddy." Suddenly the peace of the winter night was broken. She could feel her father's disappointment with her, even with his arm around her holding her tight. "Oh Daddy! I'm sorry!"

"I know, honey. And that's good. It is good to know how often we disappoint God. He wants us to be good and kind and helpful. And, instead, we're often selfish and greedy and mean."

"Not you, Daddy. Or Mommy, either. You're always good."

"No, Susan, you're wrong there. Daddy gets selfish and mean sometimes. You may not think so, but it's true. We all do. It is why Jesus came."

"What do you mean?"

"We all disappoint God by doing things we shouldn't do, or thinking things we shouldn't. Or not being helpful and generous when we should. We call that sin. Have you ever heard that word before?"

"Sin? Yes ... it means ... it means to do bad things."

"Yes, to do bad things. Or a better way to say it is to fall short. We fall short of being the good people God wants us to be."

"What does that have to do with Jesus being born in a barn?"

He chuckled. "Great question! Because we all fall short and disappoint God, He decided that, since we'd never make it on our own, that He would come to us. And that's just what He did. He came to earth as a tiny baby, born in a stable. Can you imagine that? God came to us, because we would never make it otherwise."

"So Baby Jesus was God?"

"Very good, Susan! He was ... He is ... God who came to earth a long time ago and was laid in a manger. He grew up to sacrifice Himself because of our sins. But that is a story for another day, at Easter time. Right now, I'd like you to think about God being willing to come to earth, and to be born in a smelly, dirty stable like this one. That's why I'm here in this goat barn on Christmas Eve."

The silence was broken by a screeching sound a long way off. Susan knew it was a screech owl, because her mother had taught her what that scary sound was one night. Her memory of that night suddenly came back vividly. That was the night she had shoved her brother because he had scattered the puzzle pieces she was trying to put together. Jeffie's fat little fingers had slung the pieces all over the family room before she could stop him. She had been so angry that she had pushed him hard. And he had fallen down and bumped his head on the floor. Oh, how he had cried! It took Mommy forever to get him to calm down. And Mommy had been angry with her and had sent Susan to bed before she could even kiss Mommy and Daddy good night. She had been lying in her bed crying when she heard the screech owl. It had frightened her so, and Mommy had come in and comforted her and held her close. She remembered how mean she had been to Jeffie, and how much she wanted Mommy to forgive her. And the great sense of relief when Mommy had hugged her and told her about the screech owl and had stayed with her until she had fallen asleep.

"Mommy loves me, doesn't she, Daddy?"

"Yes, honey, of course she does. And I love you. And, even better, God loves you."

"But sometimes I'm pretty mean, huh?"

"Yes, Susan, that's true. But it is also true of me and everybody else."

"I guess I'm sort of like this barn."

"What do you mean, Susan? How are you like this barn?"

"Well, it's sort of like I'm dirty … like you said, and smelly. And a bath won't fix it."

He thought about what his daughter had said. "Yes, Susan, all of us are little like this barn – dark and dirty and smelly."

"But, even so, Baby Jesus was born in a barn like this."

Susan's eyes had adjusted to the light just enough that she could make out her father's face. He was looking down at her, with his soft eyes that she loved so much. She looked up into his face, searching for what he was thinking.

Daddy kissed her forehead. "Susan, you are a very smart young lady. You're exactly right. Baby Jesus was born in a barn like this. And He wants to be in our lives, even though our lives are a lot like this barn, dirty and smelly. If He was willing to be born in a stable, wouldn't He be willing to come into the heart of someone he loved who wasn't perfect, someone like me? Or you?"

"Would He?"

"Oh, yes, Susan, He would! He would! Would you like Jesus to be in your heart?"

"Yes, Daddy, I would. Even though I'm not good enough."

"No one is, Susan. But He loves us anyway. You need to talk to Jesus, to pray to Him. Tell Him you're sorry for the mean things you've done, and that you want to do better. Tell

Him you're glad he was born in a stable, and that you'd like Him to come into your heart as well. Tell Him how much you love Him, and how grateful you are that He came to Earth."

The young girl knelt down beside the hay bale, just as her Mommy had taught her to kneel beside her bed each night. She did not pray out loud, but there was no mistaking the sincerity, the earnestness of her prayer. When she had finished she looked up at her daddy, tears running down her cold cheeks. Her tears were mirrored in the tears in her father's eyes. He laid his hands on her head. He didn't speak, but the question in his eyes was unmistakable.

"Yes," she whispered. "Yes. Baby Jesus is here." She placed her hand on her heart. "I feel ... I feel ..." Words failed her.

"Come here, my darling." He scooped her up in his strong arms and held her close. "Welcome to the family, Susan. Welcome to the family."

The screech owl called again, farther away. To Susan, he sounded disappointed, as if it had not been a good night for hunting.

"Let's go and tell your mother what has happened," said her Daddy. "OK?"

"You bet!" said Susan. She placed her smaller hand in his bigger one and they walked out of the barn toward the gate.

For a moment she looked at Mr. Austin's house over the hill. Somehow it looked too lit up, too fancy. She turned and looked back at the goat barn, the shadowy lumps of the goats still chewing their cud in the dark. "Now that," she said, "is a good place for a King."

Her Daddy laughed and swung her up onto his shoulder as he often did. "And so is this," he said, patting her heart. "So is this!"

The lights of home never looked so warm, so inviting. She could see Mommy's silhouette moving back and forth in the kitchen window. The stars seemed even brighter than before. Was it possible, she wondered, that she could see their colors? Some were intensely white, but others seemed to have a blue cast, and some even seemed tinted with crimson. And, could it be, that she heard the faint sounds of angels singing?

Think on These Things

1. What makes this story different from the others in **Lightly Salted Stories**?

2. How does this story make you feel? Uncomfortable? Glad? Angry? Indifferent? Explore your feelings about this story. Why do you feel the way you do?

3. What do you know about what is traditionally called the Christmas Story? What are the basic elements that you know? Why do people say that Baby Jesus was born in a stable? What do we know specifically about the circumstances of Jesus's birth as described in the Bible in Luke chapter 2?

4. In this story, the uncleanness of the goat barn is used as a metaphor for something else. What is the goat barn a metaphor for? Does the metaphor work, or does it stretch things too much? Why?

5. What do you think of Susan's father's explanation of the purpose for Jesus being born on earth? Does this explanation make sense to you or not? Why do you hold that opinion?

6. Contrast the Christmas lights that Susan sees on Mr. Austin's house to the stars she sees in the skies. How can these two kinds of lights represent two different views of Christmas? Is one a more authentic expression of Christmas than the other? Justify your answer.

7. A screech owl appears twice in this story. What might the screech owl represent?

8. What do you think Susan prayed as she knelt in the goat barn? What did her father suggest she say to God? Do you agree with Susan's father's suggestions? Why or why not?

9. In the story, a change seems to have taken place in Susan after her prayer. What change is that? Have you experienced a similar change? What happened?

The Road to Hell

"Wagons comin', Pa." The youth hardly paused as he shoveled load after load of gravel and dirt into the sluice. His eyes and ears were sharper than the old man's, and he had heard the rumble of the wheels even above the roar of the water in the creek.

The old man struggled to straighten his back. He used the handle of the shovel as a crutch and squinted out across the valley. "Yep. I see 'em, Lishe. Looks like settlers, headin' west."

Both men leaned on the handles of their shovels and watched the slow progress of the wagons down the trail.

It was a hot day. Clear sky, so clear the blue made your eyes hurt to look at it. Instead the men had been concentrating on their work, separating the metal that would not tarnish from the tailings and the dirt and gravel. It has been a good day – several nuggets the size of beans, and one larger, about the size of Lishe's thumb.

The wagons rolled along the stream. There were three of them, accompanied by several outriders on horses. The reins of the lead wagon were in the hands of a youngish man with nice clothes. His rifle was propped within easy reaching distance against the buckboard. He wore a six-shooter in a holster on his hip, as did most of the other men in the group. A young woman, bonnet off and hair flowing free in the breeze, sat beside him.

"Whoa," said the driver, pulling on the reins.

"Afternoon, friend," called out the old man. "Stop and rest a spell." He squinted up at the newcomers. "Name's Eli. This here's m'son, Lishe. You'd be welcome to water yer horses, if'n you like." Lishe tipped his hat.

The driver sprang down off of the wagon with a nimble grace, grabbing his rifle as his did, so that, when he landed, he had the rifle in the crook of his arm. "Thank you sir, that's quite kindly of you," he said. His manner was almost casual, with an easy air that was betrayed only by his quick and penetrating eyes. "The horses could use a drink. But we'll be moving on. We intend to make Wide Gap by nightfall."

The other settlers began unloading and allowing the horses to wade into the ford in the creek.

"I didn't catch your name," said Eli.

"I didn't give it." The young man laughed. "But, if you care, I'm called Adam Johnson. This is my wife of two months, Evelyn." The young woman nodded to Eli and Lishe.

"Well, pleased to meet you both," said Eli. "And congratulations to you, Mrs. Johnson.

Marriage is a mighty fine thing. Headin' west, are ye?"

The young man laughed again. "You're a quick one, Mister. Three loaded wagons, rolling along the trail, headed toward the setting sun. There could be another explanation, but any gambler would bet we're settlers heading for the western frontier."

Eli just leaned against his shovel. Lishe was eyeing the rifle held so casually in Johnson's arm, and the firepower he saw all around him.

"And I believe," said Johnson, stepping toward Eli, "that you gentlemen are looking for gold." Lishe took a step forward, too, as the newcomer approached his Pa.

"Shore 'nuff," said Eli. He seemed unconcerned about the fact that he and Lishe were outnumbered by more than five to one, and outgunned one hundred percent. Lishe's heart beat in his chest against the small leather pouch that hung on a rawhide cord around the his neck. He had to concentrate not to reach for it under his shirt to reassure himself it was there. Doing so would surely give its presence away. He and his Pa had worked too hard to gather the gold that snuggled there against his heart. He didn't want to lose it to this brash Eastern newcomer.

"We bin sluicin' for the metal that never fades, never tarnishes, never loses its value.

The metal that can be tested by fire and prove hitself true."

Johnson threw back his head and laughed again. This time it was a full out belly laugh. "Mister, if I thought you had something of value, I'd make sure it left with me." Even as he smiled, his eyes became like flint rocks, and Lishe believed him. Johnson never moved his face, but flicked the six shooter out of its holster, twirled it twice, and reholstered it, so quickly that Lishe, for a moment, wasn't sure what he'd seen.

"Now, Mr. Johnson," said Eli, "we are a'sluicin' for gold, and sometimes, by the Lord's providence, we are fortunate enough to find some. And hit is the genuine article. You're welcome to set up camp here for the night and give it a try. Lishe and me, we don't aim to get rich. We put a lot of work into the gold we do find. But, like I said, hit is the genuine article." Lishe glanced at his Pa. What was he thinking, inviting these folks to spend the night? They might both wind up dead, and the little leather sack against his heart in the possession of this ruffian. They had no guns, didn't think they needed them. They'd just come out here to pan a little gold and then head back to the homestead before the seasons turned. Now this fellow was making threats, and backing it up with a display of weapon prowess.

"That's a kind offer," said Johnson. "But, like I said, if I thought for a moment you had something I wanted, it would soon be mine." He drew the six shooter again with a fluid movement that made Lishe's stomach quiver. He sighted along the barrel at a pebble some fifty yards off. "But you see, Mr. Eli, I'm a geologist by training. Educated in Boston. I know my rock formations. And I know that anything you think you've found is merely iron pyrite." He turned, the six shooter still in his hand, and rather carelessly pointed it at the two men. "That's fool's gold, Mr. Eli. fool's gold."

"Clearly you be an educated man, Mr. Johnson. I can see that, shore 'nuff. But, in this case, I think you got it wrong. There's true metal in this stream. The genuine article."

Please, thought Lishe. Please, Pa, don't make me show it to him. Don't make me empty this little leather pouch out into my hands and show this man that we have something worth having. Worth killing for, if you're a man like this fellow.

Eli didn't ask for the pouch. Instead, he squinted at the newcomer and asked, "Son, go ahead and put the gun away. You won't be needin' that. But let me ask you, what are your aims? What do you and Mrs. Johnson hope for, as you're headin' west?"

Johnson holstered his gun. And, for the first time, Evelyn Johnson spoke. "Children." It was almost a whisper. "And a house. A nice big house to raise a family. And cattle."

"Yes, indeed," chimed in her husband. "lots of cattle. I'm no fool, Mr. Eli. I intend to strike it rich. All of us do." He swung his arms wide to indicate the group of settlers, now getting the horses back into position after their long drink.

"Well, I'm mighty glad to hear that," said Eli. "Everyone should have goals. 'Course now, I've done told you, the genuine article is right here in this water. I'd be pleased to show you how to sluice for it. It ain't hard."

"No, Mr. Eli. Thank you, but no. I won't be lured into a fool's errand. I know these rock formations. I've studied this geology. There is no gold here. We'll be moving on to Wide Gap and beyond."

"I wish you'd change your mind. But, if you're determined to go yer way, do you mind if I give you a piece of advice?"

"Advice? From a fool's gold prospector?" He turned away, but his wife laid a hand on his arm and he turned back. "All right, Mr. Eli, what advice?"

"Thank you, Mrs. Johnson." Eli acknowledged the young woman's role in giving him a chance to speak to her husband. "What I'm about to say is very important. You might say hit is a matter of life an' death."

"Come now, Mr. Eli. We're educated people. What can you possibly know that would help us?"

"Well, Mr. Johnson, in a few miles, just after you pass a rock that looks like a mule on your right and a clump of mesquite trees on your left, you'll come to a fork in the trail. Now the main trail, the left fork, the one most traveled, leads you to Wide Gap, where you say you're a'goin'. But the small fork to the right – hit don't look like much of a trail – why, hit's the one you want. Hit's kinda narrow in places, and hard to get through, but, if you'll take my advice, the narrow trail is the one you want."

"Very interesting." It was clear from his eyes that he was going to ignore the advice. He helped his wife up onto the wagon and then turned before he mounted. "Thank you for the advice, Mr. Eli. And good luck on your search for iron pyrite."

"Mr. Johnson, I'm a'beggin' you to hear me. Take the right fork, the narrow trail. You don't want to go through Wide Gap. Many's the people that have gone that way, and hit don't do no good."

"Mr. Eli, I have about as much faith in that advice as I do in your ability to find gold in that water there." He swung up into the seat beside his wife, carefully leaning the rifle against the seat where it would be in easy reach.

"Mrs. Johnson," Eli turned his appeal to the wife. "Please help your husband to see that Wide Gap is not the way to go. You'll pardon me for sayin', ma'am, but they've put a town in the desert on the west side of Wide Gap. And they've named that town, an', well, beggin' your pardon, ma'am, they've named that town Hell."

Mrs. Johnson colored slightly at the sound of the word, and Mr. Johnson's eyes became flinty again. " I find that comment offensive, Mr. Eli. I'll thank you not to mention that word in the presence of my wife and these other women." He slapped the reins on the horses' backs. "Heyaa! Giddyup! Mr. Eli!" he called as the wheels started their creaky rumbling. "Mr. Eli, I think you're a fool on a fool's errand. We're going to Wide Gap and we're going to make our fortune. And we don't need advice from the likes of you. Good-day, sir!" And the entire wagon train began its ponderous movement toward Wide Gap.

Lishe and Eli watched them go.

Both men went back to work, tossing shovel full after shovel full into the sluice, watching for the bright sparkle that meant another nugget to add to the pouch around Lishe's neck.

"Pa," he said tentatively, after a bit. "If that man had made you give the gold to him, would you 'a let him have it?"

126

"Yes son, I would."

"'Cause it ain't worth gettin' killed over?"

"Well, in a way. More'n that, hit might 'a saved his life."

"Saved his life, Pa? How could gold have saved his life?"

"Lishe, you ain't never been over Wide Gap, but I have. I know what it's like over there. I weren't pulling that Easterner's leg – there really is a town over there called Hell. An' it deserves its name, too. That feller may think he's takin' the easy road, but, in the end, he'll wish he'd 'a listened to us."

They both returned to their work until the sky to the West began to redden. "Time to head for the cabin, Lishe," said Pa. The men gathered their tools and headed back up the trail.

"Still," said Lishe. "I'm glad we have the gold."

"Yep. That's right, Lishe. But there's plenty to share, don't ya think?"

Lishe knew the value of the gold in the pouch around his neck. This amount of metal had brought them a fortune at the assayer's last year, and, to his eye, it looked like the gold they now had weighed even more. Yes, they had more than they needed. "I reckon, Pa. We've got plenty to share."

The Johnson party spent the night at the rock that looked like a mule in the shade of the clump of mesquite trees. In the morning, Mr. Johnson even took a look at the narrow trail to the right, but, when it came time to get the wagon train moving, he led the party to the left, along the wider, smoother trail. They made Wide Gap by the sixth day, but had trouble with one of their wagons – it lost a wheel and they had to spend half a day repairing it.

The western slopes of Wide Gap were certainly more arid, and Johnson instructed his party to conserve water. The bleached carcasses of cattle and mules did not cheer the settlers. By the fourteenth day, the party was almost out of water and pushing across an acrid, desiccated plain, parched and scanning the horizon for any sign of a watering hole. Old Mrs. Neeley passed on the twentieth day since they had seen the prospectors. They held a brief burial service and pressed on into the burning sun. On the twenty-eighth day they made a decision to kill one of the horses for food because several of the party were failing. It didn't do a lot of good; they buried six more of their party over the next four days.

After that, things got really bad. On the thirty-nineth day, Mrs. Johnson died, leaving only Mr. Johnson and one other man to struggle on alone.

The next day, Mr. Johnson spotted an image on the horizon. As it got closer, he realized it was a watering hole. He and the other man began to run with the little strength they had left. They reached the hole and dove into the water. It was wet but, as they gulped mouthful after mouthful, Johnson's geologist training told him what he was doing. The water had a distinct alkali taste – it was most certainly poison. As he crawled out onto the edge of the water hole, he spotted the sign he had missed earlier. In crude letters, someone had scrawled, "Welcome to Hell."

Think on These Things

1. In this story there are two different perspectives on life, that of the prospector and his son, and that of the Easterners heading west. Describe and compare these two views of life.

2. Before the story came to its conclusion, what did you think would happen to the Easterners? What clues in the story made you think that?

3. If you could honestly put yourself in the place of the Easterners, what would you have thought about the old prospector's warnings? Would you have heeded them? What reasons were there to believe his warnings might be true? What reasons were there to not heed his warnings and to go ahead through Wide Gap?

4. Why do you think Mr. Johnson was so convinced that the prospectors could not be finding real gold, only fool's gold or iron pyrite? What might have blinded him to the truth?

5. How do you think the story would have played out if Johnson had chosen to search among the prospectors' possessions? Write a different ending to the story in which Johnson discovers that Lishe has a sack of gold nuggets tied around his neck. How would the prospectors respond? How would

the others in Johnson's party have reacted
and what would they have done?

6. What do you think gold could represent in
   this story? Is it important that Eli says he
   would have willingly given the gold to the
   men? What might have motivated that
   comment? How is it symbolic where Lishe
   keeps the gold?

7. Were you suspicious that the gold that Lishe
   carries was not actually real, but was fool's
   gold as Johnson would have predicted? Is
   there anything in the story that leads you to
   believe that the gold is real or false? What is
   your conclusion – is it real gold? Why or why
   not?

The CEO and the Intern

William Green answered the intercom on his mahogany desk. "Yes, Miss Jensen?"

"The new intern is here, Mr. Green. Susan Wagoner?"

"Yes, right. I've been expecting her. Bring her right in."

He stood up and straightened his tie. He turned to the bank of windows looking out over the Ohio River and downtown Louisville. Quite a view. He never tired of it.

There was a soft tap at the door and it opened. Miss Jensen stepped in followed by an attractive young woman in her early to mid twenties. She's dressed appropriately, thought Green as he turned to greet her. Conservative suit, the skirt showing a nice set of legs punctuated by heels tall enough to be interesting, not so tall as to be ostentatious. Her hair was an intriguing copper color, pulled back at the nape. Nice, he thought to himself. Very nice.

"Mr. Green, this is Susan Wagoner."

"Hello, Susan." He strode across the room and offered his hand. "Welcome to Green-Leader."

She took his hand. Firm grip. That's good, he noted. Confident. "How do you do, Mr. Green? I'm very glad to meet you."

"Likewise, likewise! We're delighted to welcome you to Green-Leader as our newest intern."

"Can I get you anything?" Miss Jensen was hovering near the door.

"How about it, Susan? Can we get you a drink?"

He saw the question in her eyes, but she said, after a pause, "No. No thank you. I'm fine."

"Very good then. I think that will be all, Miss Jensen." Miss Jensen closed the door behind her. "Come over here, Susan, and take in this view." Susan walked over to the bank of windows with him and turned to look out over the city. "Quite a scene, isn't it?"

"It is breathtaking. As many times as I've been across the bridge, I've never seen it from up so high."

"We're on top of the world here. Or at least on top of Louisville. Green-Leader is an important company in the local economy."

"Oh I know! And may I say how grateful I am to have been given this opportunity to be an intern here? I'm so looking forward to the experience and to what I will learn here."

"Your resume at U. of L. was impressive. We definitely thought you were the right person for the experience."

"Thank you, Mr. Green. You can imagine how thrilled I was to learn that, not only had I been granted an internship at Green-Leader, but that I would be working for the CEO himself."

He laughed. "I guess the Green name has been around for a few years." He gestured to the row of portraits on the far wall.

"Are those ..." She was drawn to the paintings, much like a gallery goer is drawn to the art on display.

"Yes, those are my ancestors. I'm the sixth generation Green to head up this company."

She examined the first Green, Jedediah according to the brass label below the painting, in his quaint 18th century frilled collar. Each subsequent portrait spoke of changing men's fashion through the decades, both in dress and hair style. Some were Greens, others had the surname Leader. The Green's particularly were linked by a clear similarity of facial structure: high cheek bones, thin lips, and small, dark eyes. "This is quite remarkable," she said.

"Yes, we've been in the bourbon business since 1792. Old Jedediah Green didn't have our modern production methods or our comfortable offices — he made his distillation outside of a log cabin — but he sure knew how to make good bourbon. And we've upheld the tradition ever since."

"Remarkable!" She glanced around the room again, at the panoramic view from the top floor of the Green-Leader Building, at the huge mahogany desk, at the modern stainless steel sculptures contrasting with the row of patriarchal portraits. She smiled at him. "I'm really looking forward to working here."

"Then we had best be discussing what your duties will be during your internship with us, hadn't we?" She smiled again. "Why don't you sit here ..." He indicated one of the leather guest chairs. "And we'll get started."

The days turned into weeks. She's really on the ball, thought Green to himself. Quite a find. The university didn't always send them this talented an intern. Need to remember to have Jensen send a note of thanks to the Provost, he thought.

Sometimes Susan worked in his office at the second desk. Sometimes she worked in the outer office with Miss Jensen. Sometimes he sent her to work on other floors with other departments within the Green-Leader building. Sometimes he even sent her out to one of the distilleries. She was a quick learner, asking sharp and insightful questions, quickly grasping the interplay of strategies, processes, profits and corporate culture.

During her sixth week, they were looking at the galley proofs for a new marketing campaign. The bourbon was to be bottled in a newly-designed carafe, intended to appeal to younger audiences. Green wanted to get Susan's insights into how the campaign would be received by her demographic.

"So, what do you think, Susan? Will young people your age notice this ad?"

She cocked her head and looked at it critically. The image showed a young couple, glasses in their hands, other young couples in the background, smiling and laughing. "Yes, I think so. The girl is attractive, but not so attractive as to turn young female customers off." She grinned at Green. "Competition, you know. But I would guess that young men will like the hint of cleavage." She pointed to the young man. "He's gorgeous, with that blonde hair and bright blue eyes. Girls will love him. And I'd say young men will identify with him, want to be like him." She paused for effect. "And drink the same bourbon he drinks."

"Exactly! That's what the marketing department was going for. You nailed it!"

"Mr. Green, how old would you say these people are?"

"The models we used in the shoot? I couldn't guess. Early twenties, I'd say."

"That's what I was thinking. Mr. Green, what is Green-Leader's policy on drinking and young people."

"Oh, obviously we want young people to drink responsibly, of course." He pointed to the text in small print toward the bottom of the ad. Please drink responsibly, it said. "Why do you ask?"

"Well, the people in this ad seem quite young. I was just wondering if there was an age below which you didn't want people drinking our bourbon."

He thought a moment. "I would say there is. I mean ... it has to be at the right time. After all, our bourbon is fairly potent stuff. I should ask you ... what do you think of it?"

"I, well ..." Her face colored slightly. "I have to confess, Mr. Green. I've not actually tried it."

"Really? Really?" He was not angry, just puzzled. "Yet you work here? And you haven't actually tried ..."

"I guess that's one of the reasons I asked you about the age of the couple in the ad. Is there an age below which ... you see, Mr. Green, I'll turn 21 tomorrow."

"Well, well! Quite a milestone! Congratulations!" He could tell she was waiting for something else. "Will you be in to work tomorrow? We must celebrate!"

"No, tomorrow I have classes all day. Kind of a crazy way to celebrate my 21st birthday, huh? But my mom will be coming up from Bowling Green to celebrate with me on Saturday."

"Oh, that's good. Sorry you won't be here on the big day, though. Happy birthday, in advance! Don't go too crazy ... you say you've never tried our bourbon?"

"No, I haven't. But I was wondering if ..."

Again he paused. This was more complex than he thought. "Susan, in many ways you've become like a daughter to me. Your work here at Green-Leader has been remarkable. You're smart, articulate, pretty — there will be a place for you here when you graduate, if you want it. I hope you will. And much as I like making bourbon, perhaps your 21st birthday isn't the time to start drinking it."

"But that's what I want to know! When is the right time?"

"When it's right. You'll know."

"My grandfather was an alcoholic." She said it quietly, almost to herself. "So was my dad. That's what caused him and mom to break up."

"I'm sorry to hear that."

She looked up at him. "Mr. Green? Why do we produce something that isn't ..."

"It isn't that, Susan. Many people enjoy our bourbon very much. But we just trust that people will drink responsibly ..."

"Perhaps my 21st birthday is the time." She turned abruptly and left the room.

He was driving in to work the next morning but had to detour his usual route because of an accident. He parked the Porsche in his space in the parking garage and took the elevator to the 21st floor, said good morning to Miss Jensen, and hung his coat and hat on the rack. The late February sun was casting a rosy glow over the city and gleaming off the waters of the Ohio, peppered by early morning barge traffic. He could see the flashing red lights near the accident directly below him, the accident that had inconvenienced his commute that morning.

Below, the officer working the accident noted that the air bag had deployed in the small Corolla, but that the single passenger did not appear to have survived. Skid marks indicated a high rate of speed before leaving the street, jumping the curb, and colliding with a telephone pole. "Not wearing a seat belt," said the officer.

The coroner confirmed it. "Deceased at the scene," his report noted. "We'll want a blood alcohol level. I suspect alcohol. How about you, Jimmy?"

The officer sniffed the air. "Definitely," he said, and shook his head.

The two EMTs driving the ambulance that would transport the body to the morgue could not help but remark on the stunning copper color of the young victim's hair. "Look, Bob," said one of them. He pointed to the ID card from her personal effects. "She was an intern at Green-Leader."

"Yep," said Bob. "This makes the ... what? ... the third Green-Leader intern in five years with a fatal DUI."

"Third in five years," he confirmed. He flipped on the light as Bob eased the ambulance out into traffic. He didn't turn on the siren as there was no rush for this run.

Think on These Things

1. With which character, Mr. Green or Susan, did you have more empathy? Why?

2. What emotions did you feel at the end of the story? Were you sad? Angry? Disappointed? Frustrated? Describe your emotions and explain why you had those emotions.

3. While few details are provided in the story, imagine what Mr. Green's childhood might have been like. What would he have experienced? How was he prepared (if at all) for his job as the CEO of Green-Leader? Write a few paragraphs describing Mr. Green's growing up years, as you imagine them, and how those experiences might have shaped him into the corporate leader he is in the story.

4. Do the same thing for Susan. What do you imagine her childhood was like? What prompted her to attend the University and to seek an internship at Green-Leader? What were her goals in life? Write a few paragraphs about Susan's background and how that shaped her as the intern she is in the story.

5. What about the tragedy that ensued? Try to reconstruct Susan's movements and thoughts between when she left Green-Leader and the accident that took her life. Where did she go? What did she do? Who did she

interact with? What actions led to the
accident?

6. Think about responsibility. Do you think
Susan had any responsibility for the accident
in which she died? Why or why not? Were
there other people that had responsibility for
the accident as well? We often use the term
"accident victim." Was Susan a victim here?
In what way?

7. What role, if any, did Mr. Green have in the
accident? Did he have any responsibility for
the accident? What about his company,
Green-Leader? Did the company have any
responsibility for the accident? Defend your
answers.

8. How do you respond to the statement Mr.
Green made, "We just trust that people will
drink responsibly." Do you agree with that
position he took on behalf of his company? Is
it a reasonable position to take? What role, if
any, do organizations, not individuals, have
in the responsibility people take for their own
actions?

9. You might think this story is only about use
and abuse of alcohol. But look a bit deeper.
If it is a story about the roles of individuals
and organizations in society, what other
scenarios could have been used to examine
the subject of responsibility? What other
substances or activities that some people
enjoy, but that may also lead to harm, might
have been used equally effectively? Sketch

out a story outline that raises the same questions, but that uses a different scenario.

Frontier Life

Zeb wasn't sure if he was dreaming or if it was really happening. He was in a canoe, Cherokee by the looks of it, going downstream. He reached for the paddle, but there wasn't any. Dirty redskin. Probably stole the paddle.

He gripped the sides of the canoe as the swift current propelled him along. Luckily there weren't a lot of rocks in the river, or the canoe would have busted up for sure. But the banks were steep, and he would not have been able to get out of the river, even if he had a paddle. Zeb was in trouble.

Downstream he could just see a tree, tilted out over the water. If it were low enough, he might be able to grab on to it and swing out of the canoe. As it got closer he realized it would probably be too high. Then he spotted a man, lying on the trunk of the tree out over the water. The man was calling to him.

"Grab my hand!" he said. "Let me save you from the great water."

Zeb realized it was an Indian. The canoe raced closer in the fast current.

The Indian reached down so that Zeb would be able to grab his hand. "Grab hold!" The voice was more urgent this time. "Thunder water ahead! Me save you!"

Zeb could see the Indian's piercing black eyes, now, he was so close. He could see his black hair, tied into braids. He could see the mottled bark of the sycamore tree where the Indian hung, reaching for him with his outstretched hand.

"Get away, Injun!" Zeb spat as the canoe sped under the tree. "I don't need no redskin's help." He turned to see the Indian gazing at him as he passed by in his runaway canoe.

"Thunder water ahead," the Indian called. "Danger!"

It was then that Zeb first heard the deep rumble of the falls. The noise grew deafening as the canoe approached – from the way the water dropped away he knew it was a big one. The mist boiling off beyond the edge of the water told him of the rocks below the falls. He gripped the gunwales of the canoe ... and woke up.

At first Zeb wasn't sure where he was. The dream had been so vivid. He smelled the chill of the fast-moving water, heard the pounding of the falls, felt the giddy tossing of the canoe with no paddle to steer. The Indian in the tree was vivid in his memory, too. "Let me save you," he had said as he reached out his hand. Indians! Couldn't trust them. Probably just a trick.

As Zeb became more conscious, he became aware of a whole different set of senses. His mouth tasted like dirt. He smelled smoke. He was cold. His head felt like it was being smashed between two rocks.

He opened his eyes and realized he was lying-face down on the ground, his mouth pressed into the ground. He tried to sit up, but his head was pounding too much. He was afraid for a moment he might be sick, but that passed and he was able to struggle up on his hands and knees. He sat down on the dirt, squinting out through the trees. It was early morning, by the looks of it. The mist was just lifting as shafts of sunlight angled down through the maples and hickories.

He knew those trees – they were the trees in front of his cabin. He craned his head around behind him and cried out at the sight. His cabin, where he and Patience and little Isaac lived, was a smoldering ruin. Burned to the ground! Without even thinking, he knew what had happened. He'd heard that the Shawnee had been raiding up and down the Warrior's Path. They'd come to his cabin – he didn't remember a thing about it, but how could he? He'd probably escaped with his life. Instinctively he reached for his hair. Still there. He'd heard of people being scalped and living to tell about it.

Suddenly he thought of Patience and baby Isaac! He staggered to his feet, squinting his eyes against the pain in his head. The walls of the cabin were mostly standing, although there were several places where the fire was still active. He ignored the occasional pop from the burning logs as he tried to gain access to the interior. The roof had collapsed and burned, covering over what little was left of his possessions with ash and charred wood. Then he saw it – the thing he dreaded to see. Patience's boot was sticking out from under a burned roof shake. He pushed it aside with his toe, and saw her leg. Suddenly he was down on his knees, ignoring the embers, shoving logs and shakes aside to reach her. It was Patience, all right, with little Isaac in her arm. Dead. His dear Patience, dead.

He let out a groan and beat his chest again and again, giving over to sobs that wracked his body.

It was later in the morning when he composed himself a bit. He would need to give her a descent burial. He looked around for the storehouse – it hadn't been burned. He found a wooden shovel and commenced to digging a grave in the middle of the Lady Slipper flowers that Patience had loved so much. The ground wasn't too hard and he was able to dig a nice final resting place.

Then he gathered up her body, tenderly wrapping her in a blanket from the store house, holding her to him one last time before he laid her in the ground. He did the same with little Isaac, not yet one year old, laying him on his mother's breast. He felt he should pray, but didn't know what to say. "Lord," he said. "Take care of them. They're all I had." He filled in the grave and found a flat stone from the creek to mark the site.

As he was collecting other stones to lay on the grave to keep animals from digging up the bodies, he spotted it. It was barely visible beside the smoldering cabin ruins. He knelt down and unearthed it. An arrow. A Shawnee arrow.

Suddenly the pain in his head was pushed aside by rage. He knew who was responsible for the deaths of his wife and son and he knew what he had to do.

People up and down the frontier talked about Zeb after that. How he'd gone on his own personal war path. How he'd given up living like a descent human being and taken to living in caves or just out in the open. How he'd sooner kill an Indian than eat. Some folks said he was stirring up the Shawnee, making the uneasy truce between the white man and the red man fray around the edges. Other folks were glad for Zeb's rage. He was doing what, perhaps, they wished they had the courage to do. "The only good Indian's a dead Indian," they said. Some helped him on his way – giving him powder for his powder horn, or a mess of grub to eat, or moonshine. Zeb was as glad to get a jar of 'shine as he was to get anything else.

Zeb was a tracker. If he ran across an Indian sign, he'd follow the trail wherever it would lead. He'd take a pull or two on his wineskin, and then he'd take off. It was uncanny how keen his senses were. He could see every bent twig, spot every scuffed leaf. He could smell the faintest whiff of smoke or pemmican hanging in the air where the Indians had passed. And, when he was close, he could feel their presence. Like as not he'd find an Indian or two, out hunting or going about whatever business Injuns had running up and down the woods. And then he'd ambush them – shoot first, and then move in fast with his knife. In his rage he seemed unstoppable, and the Indians paid the price.

It was in the fall of the year that Zeb met his match. He was trailing a group of Indians, moving fast and heading north. He reckoned there were eight or ten of them, judging from the way the leaves on the forest floor were disturbed. It was hard to tell with Indians, as they traveled in single file to disguise their numbers.

He caught up with them just as twilight was beginning to fall. He smelled them more than saw them, knew they were close. He ducked down behind a rock outcrop and reconnoitered the situation. He was able to roll under a hemlock tree for cover, then work his way over to another rock outcrop a little higher up. From there he was able to slide out onto the top of the rock and look down to where the Indians were. There were three of them; he must have overestimated their numbers because of the volume of falling maple and sycamore leaves. They had lit a small campfire and were preparing to heat some dried meat from their kit. Shadowed as he was by the undergrowth in the deepening twilight, the Indians were completely unaware of his presence.

How to take all three of them? He could certainly kill one with his rifle, but he'd be hard pressed to reload and take a second one before they would be up to the rock outcropping and be on top of him. He knew he could take a second one with his knife, but the third one was a problem. Zeb took a swig from his skin and thought of Patience and baby Isaac. This was for them. He drew out the arrow he had found that day that the cabin had burned and fingered it again, rolling it through his fingers. Same triangular shape, definitely Shawnee, same yellow color with a white streak running through the flint. "Oh Patience ... if only ..."

He made a decision. Because it was a way up from the campfire to the top of the rock he was on, he just might be able reload and get off a second shot before they were on top of him. Then he'd finish off third one with his knife.

He carefully laid out his rod, his powder horn, and his second bullet, so they'd be ready. Then he loaded the first round, tamping the powder down before inserting the bullet. Quietly he got into a kneeling position and took aim on the Indian closest to him.

The flint struck home; there was that delay while the fire worked its way into the chamber, and then, boom, the gun went off and Zeb saw, through the smoke, that the first Indian was down. He grabbed his powder horn to reload, but he never got the chance.

There were other Indians, ones he should have know would be there. They had circled around behind him and had him before he could even get the horn to the end of the still heated gun. Zeb saw them out of the corner of his eye – six of them at least – before a tomahawk smashed into the back of his head and he went down.

When Zeb came to, his head hurt like thunder, but he was alive. His hands and feet were bound and he could dimly see the Indians gathered around the campfire. They were holding a powwow, occasionally glancing in his direction.

One of them saw that he was conscious and came over to him. He hauled Zeb roughly to his feet and propelled him over to the campfire, forcing him to kneel beside them.

The older one who seemed to be the chief addressed him. "You Zeb Indian killer." It wasn't really a question, more a statement of fact. Zeb glared at him. "You!" The chief poked him in the chest. "Zeb Indian killer."

"Yah, you dirty redskin. That's me. Zeb. I kill Indians. An' I woulda killed more of you'ns if you hadn't 'a snuck up on me." He spat on the ground beside the chief.

One of the braves raised his tomahawk and Zeb figured this was the end. Well, he'd killed as many as he could. If he could get out of this one, he'd kill more. But, if this was it, well, he'd ended the lives of as many. He wondered, briefly, if Patience would be waiting for him.

The chief raised his hand, palm out, and the brave stopped, tomahawk in the air. It was a simple gesture, but obedience was immediate. The brave put the weapon away and Zeb inwardly grinned. As long as he was alive, there was a chance. His mind began working out ways he might escape. The cords on his wrists and ankles were tight, but he began quietly working them, testing for slack and weakness.

The chief spoke at length to the other braves. Zeb only knew a word or two — "journey" and "river," maybe "three days" — he really had no idea what the chief was saying. The braves began making preparations and it became clear that they were going to bed down here for the night. Guards were posted and they pointed to where Zeb was to lay.

It was a long night. The Indians didn't seem concerned if he slept or not, so Zeb ended up watching them. They changed guard in the middle of the night so that every brave was rested. There didn't seem to be any laziness Zeb could exploit; every guard was vigilant. Zeb's thirst grew. "Give me some water, you filthy redskin!" he demanded. "Better yet, give me some of my 'shine." He pointed to his wineskin and made drinking noises. The braves were stoic and ignored him.

In the morning they give him a little water to drink and some dried corn, and then quickly they were off. The brave Zeb had shot was born between two braves. The bindings on Zeb's legs were removed, and he was tethered between two other braves. Zeb kept working on the cords around his wrist whenever his handlers were distracted.

The general direction seemed to be north. The pace was determined and unceasing. When Zeb stumbled, one of his captors pushed him to his feet and then resumed the same dogged pace.

They came to the Ohio and Zeb thought he might have a chance to escape there, but no such luck. They crossed in canoes that had must have been left as the tribe first came south. It began to ease into Zeb's mind that maybe they were heading for Chillicothe, the great Shawnee settlement.

Zeb lost count of the days. Even before his capture, one day had blurred into another, each one shot through with the desire for redskin blood. Now that he was their captive, his rage burned deeper into his soul. His life became a constant cadence of the forced march demanded by his captors and the constant plotting for escape and revenge. The image of his dead wife and son haunted his dreams; the continual striding of the thighs of the brave ahead of him filled his days as he stumbled along, trying to keep up.

At last they arrived at a large Indian village. No doubt is was Chillicothe for all the large number of men, women, children, teepees, campfires, and everything else about Indians that Zeb despised. He was tied, standing, at a stake in the center of the village where he had to endure the silent stares of his guards and of the women and children who passed by. His mouth became too dry to spit, even though he was given water and food periodically. It began to dawn on Zeb that this might truly be then end. In a way, he would have welcomed death, so that he could join Patience in the cold, hard ground. But in another way he was not willing to die –

there were so many more redskins here that needed killing for what they had done. Tied to the stake, day after day, night after night, Zeb nursed his bitterness like spark in a campfire, willing it to burst into flame at the moment when he would make his escape and continue to extract his revenge on his enemies.

One afternoon, as the shadows began to lengthen and the sun hung low in the sky, Zeb could sense that something was up. The Indians who passed by the stake where he was tied looked at him in a different way – longer, some with more curiosity, some with a burning intensity that Zeb could almost feel. Their dark eyes drilled into him, heightening his misery and bitterness.

As dusk approached, two braves came and untied him and led him to a different part of the village where a campfire was burning. The chief was seated on a stool and was dressed in his full war regalia. Gathered around him were the lead braves, standing in a semicircle with the campfire casting their dancing shadows on the walls of the teepees in the accumulating darkness. Zeb swallowed hard and wriggled against the firm grips of the men who held him captive. They held him like an ox in a yoke – escape seemed impossible.

The men brought Zeb to stand in front of the campfire, facing the chief. For many moments they just stood there, the chief's dark eyes boring a hole into Zeb's very soul, and Zeb staring defiantly back.

The chief stood, then, and the crowd that had gathered around collectively moved closer in anticipation. The chief spoke in a deep and resonating voice. Zeb could not understand a word of what was said, but it was clear that the chief was talking about him. The chief would point at Zeb as he spoke; the language was compelling and dramatic. Occasionally the crowd would respond, mostly with a grunt or a quick nod of the head. The chief paced back and forth as he spoke, his voice carrying to the darkening trees overhead. More Indians arrived to stand quietly in a circle around the campfire, listening to what their chief said.

At last, the chief sat down and motioned to one of the braves sanding behind him. The first brave stepped forward and made a speech. The chief asked the brave a question, although Zeb could not understand it, and the brave pointed directly at Zeb. The crowd murmured and Zeb understood now that he was on trial.

A second brave stepped forward, animated in his presentation. Again the chief asked a question, and the brave pointed at Zeb. A third brave stepped forward, telling a story more in gesture than in word of one man killing another man. The chief asked several questions and the brave answered them. Then the chief asked the final question and this brave, too, pointed at Zeb.

In all, seven braves stepped forward to give evidence. Each time, Zeb was indicated. Each time the crowed nodded in assent. but each time the chief's face remained stony and unreadable.

Finally, after the last brave had spoken, the chief stood. His deep voice resonated against the tree branches that overhung the assembly. He pointed at Zeb as he addressed the crowd and paced around the campfire. When he was directly in front of Zeb he turned to face him full on. The two braves on either side of Zeb pulled him up so that he stood a little straighter. The chief's eyes again pierced deep into Zeb's core.

"You, Brave-killer!" he said in English so Zeb could understand. "You kill many men. They not kill you."

Zeb stared defiantly at the chief.

"You!" The chief's voice boomed even louder. "You, Zeb Brave-killer! You kill many men."

"Yah, an' I woulda' killed more if'n you hadn't caught me!"

"You. You Brave killer. You kill many men." His voice lowered and the circle of observers leaned in to hear what he would say. "Now you die." He said it matter-of-factly.

For a moment the words hung in the darkness. There was no wind in the trees overhead. The night insects were silent. No one spoke, murmured or breathed.

Then, deep from Zebs throat began a horrific, rebellious roar. The pent-up rage that he had been nursing, tending, growing, building burst into full flame. It started deep inside him and, by the time it was past his tongue, his teeth, his lips it was a howl that focused all his hatred of the Indians and what they had done to him in a single discharge of defiance.

"Nooooo! You filthy, filthy redskins. You killed my wife! You killed my son! YOU ... " He gasped for breath. "You filthy, filthy, filthy ..." He shook his captors so hard that he managed to slip one arm away from one of them, but he was quickly recaptured. "You killed my ... wife. You killed my son!"

The chief held up his hand. Again it seemed that this simple gesture had the power to stop Zeb in his tracks.

"We no kill Zeb Brave-killer wife. We no kill boy."

"Yes you did! Yes you did! I found your arrow! I know you did it ... burned my cabin, killed Patience, killed Issac."

Again the chief simply held up his hand. "No. We no kill them. Yet you kill many braves. Now you die."

The chief pointed to a framework made of poles lashed together. With a small nod of his head, Zeb's captors began to haul him toward the structure. Zeb could only guess what torture awaited him there. He saw the ropes looped up over the cross piece twice as high as a man's head.

The crowd parted as Zeb was muscled toward the place of his execution.

"No." The voice was not the chief's. As one the crowed turned to see who would dare to challenge the chief's decree.

A young man stepped forward. He had been standing near the chief, but had not been one of the braves who had testified. His black hair was tied into braids and he had the demeanor and dress of an important member of the tribe.

"No," he said again.

The chief spoke in the language of the Shawnee. The young brave replied. The chief asked a question of the young man and the young man answered. His answer surprised the crowd; there were whispers and glances, mouths open in shock, eyebrows raised. The chief's voice became louder and he asked more questions. Each time the brave responded calmly, often with a nod of his head. His face was stoic but his eyes betrayed the intense emotion within. The conversation continued for some minutes. Then in the firelight, Zeb caught a glint off of the old chief's cheek. A single tear was coursing down his face.

Finally the chief nodded. He raised his voice and spoke to the entire assembly. While Zeb could not understand a word, he could tell that his words were deeply troubling to him, almost as if he was unwilling to say what was being said. At one point the crowd gasped; at another point they protested with shakes of their head and sounds of disapproval deep in their throat.

Finally the chief came over and stood in front of Zeb. "You Zeb Brave-killer. You kill many men. They not kill you. For this you die. But this ... " He gently pulled the young brave over so that Zeb was looking directly into his black eyes. "This my son. My first born. My chief to become." The chief paused to wipe another tear off of his cheek with the back of his wrinkled hand. "He now die. Take your place."

"What? You mean ..."

The young brave continued his intense gaze of Zeb.

"Silence!" Again the chief held up his hand. "Son take your place. This justice!" With that, he smacked his open palm with the fist of his other hand. "Now go!" He pointed out into the darkness beyond the campfire, beyond the teepees.

The men restraining Zeb instantly released Zeb and stood beside the young brave. The chief stepped forward and cut the cords that bound Zeb with his knife. "Now go!" he repeated.

Zeb looked again into the brave's dark eyes. What did he see there? Why was he doing this? "I ..." Words failed him.

"You go, Zeb Brave-killer," said the brave. "You live now." Then the brave, unbidden, began a slow death-march to the instrument of torture rigged in the trees.

Suddenly Zeb awoke, as if from a dream. He had to get away. Now was his chance!

He took a tentative step away from the chief and the braves around him. No one hindered him. He took another step. And another. It was as if they had forgotten him as they watched the young brave arrive at the structure, watched him being lashed to the cross piece, watched as the braves who had the task of carrying out the sentence hauled away on the ropes.

The last sight Zeb saw as he neared the edge of the clearing was the brave, now hanging above the crowd. Across the crowd their eyes locked for a fleeting moment, Zeb seeing the black eyes of a dying man hanging where he should have been, the brave seeing the clouded blue eyes of a man who was now on the run. The last sound Zeb heard was a woman sob.

Then he was away, running as fast as he could, tearing through the underbrush, putting as much distance as he could between him and the grizzly scene.

Later, when it seemed he had been running for hours, he tripped over a root and fell on his face. And there, lying in the dirt, he blubbered like a baby.

He lay there the rest of the night in anguish, trying and failing to come to terms with what had happened to him. Finally he slept, a dreamless sleep as still as death.

When he awoke it was already first light. The birds were singing and the rosy glow of the rising sun was shining off of the slick bare bark of the sycamores. Zeb was cold and hungry, but those were of little concern as he assessed his situation.

He had been given a reprieve. For what reason he couldn't fathom. The brave had taken his place. Why he couldn't even guess. And, come to think of it, you couldn't trust an Injun anyways. Why, they might be looking for him already. He'd been lucky to get away, that was for sure. He'd better get a move on, and cover his tracks while he was at it.

Zeb looked around. The rising sun told him which way was east, and which way he needed to go if he was going to get back south again to the settlements and away from the Shawnee.

He headed south, but not in a straight direction. He covered his tracks as best he could, using rocks where there were outcroppings and twice wading through a creek, once upstream, just to throw off any pursuit. He found a few late berries to eat to stave off the gnawing hunger and later was fortunate to find a chestnut tree with its prickly fruit lying underneath. He tied as many as he could into his shirt for later after eating his fill.

When nightfall came he found a crevice in a rock to crawl into that kept the worst of the cold away. But the weather was definitely taking a turn and Zeb knew he had better keep moving if he was going to survive.

The second day was a little better. He found a few more berries and nuts to eat. And, as he gained some high ground he took the time to climb a big white pine. He looked to the north scanning for any pursuit. He didn't see any, but he continued his careful trek southward, erasing his trail at every opportunity.

The third night he risked a small campfire between two rock outcrops, patiently rubbing dry sticks together until a tiny spark could be coaxed into a flame.

The fourth night he actually caught a small fish, made lazy by the cooling weather, with his bare hands.

Slowly but relentlessly he worked his way south. The day came that he arrived on the banks of the Ohio. He'd been thinking about this for several days, knowing that crossing the big river would be a challenge. In the end, he simply swam it. He was carried far downstream as he crossed, but he made it, hauling himself, exhausted, onto the southern bank. He now had a bit more safety from the Shawnee; so far as he knew, the Shawnee rarely ventured south of the Ohio in winter.

Zeb began to work on getting his bearings. For several days he would deliberately choose high ground to see if he could spot a familiar mountain formation. His instincts told him he was west of the white settlements so he altered his course to be southeast.

After weeks of traveling he began to have the sense that these mountains were nearer to home. They had the right shape, the right look. There were many knobs — mountains with a ring of cliffs near the top — just like there had been where he and Patience had built their cabin.

He came to a river that was almost certainly the Kentucky with its dramatic palisades and bends through the mountains. By now his moccasins were almost worn through. The weather had a real bite now, that gave him a sense of urgency. His shirt and trousers flapped in tatters around him as he walked.

Then came the day that he spotted Pilot Knob. He was sure of it, the lone mountain, separate from the others, just the right shape. He knew now that he might actually survive. Just as the snow began to fly he found the familiar Wilderness Road path that led to the fort at Boonesboro. As he banged on the gates, he clutched what was left of his shirt and tattered trousers around him. The snow was coming down in earnest as he was let in, led to a warm fire, given a blanket and a bowl of hot corn mush, welcomed home.

"Yep, 'ats him. Zeb Tate. Married my oldest cousin Hiram's second girl Patience. Ahd 'a knowed him anywheres. Looks kinda' pitiful, shore enough. But 'ats him, for shore." Old Aunt Betsy was the resident midwife, physician and gossip. She kept her wrinkled hands and hooked nose in everyone's business. For once Zeb was glad to have the familiar face and ministrations of kinfolk. Old Aunt Betsy tended to his cracked and bleeding feet, fed him bits of broth and cornmeal to coax his strength back, mopped his brow when the fever took hold of him and almost killed him. But slowly, gradually Zeb fought his way back: back to a semblance of health, back to living among his people, back to sanity.

Old Aunt Betsy kept curious folks away. Zeb had been gone a long time. His exploits as an Indian killer had become the stuff of stories told 'round the fire. And his disappearance caused speculation and wild supposition. But Old Aunt Betsy would only let a few people who had a good reason come in to see Zeb. He wasn't that strong yet, especially in his mind. But, as the early crocus started to bloom and the threat of snow seemed more distant, Zeb was able to stretch his legs and sit out on the stoop of Old Aunt Betsy's cabin where she nursed sick folks and kept her herbal medicines.

One afternoon, when the sun was shining and bringing warmth back into Zeb's body, Jeremiah Paterson stopped by. "How you feeling, Zeb?"

"I been better, Jeremiah, and that's the truth. But I'm glad to be alive."

"Ain't we all!" Jeremiah stood for a while, drawing in the sunshine.

"Care to come up and set a spell?" Jeremiah had been a good friend of Zeb's in their younger years.

"Don't care if I do, Zeb." Jeremiah stepped up on the porch and hunkered down on a stool. He leaned it back against the rough hewn logs and chinking of the cabin wall. They sat in silence for a while, gazing out at the faint green tint showing in some of the bare trees.

"Warmer weather's a'comin'," said Jeremiah.

"Yep. And I don't mind tellin' you that I'll be glad to see it." He shivered involuntarily, remembering the cold of the Ohio river, remembering the Indian in the clearing, lifted up above the crowd, and his piercing black eyes.

"Zeb," Jeremiah said quietly. "What happened to you?" It wasn't said with the idle curiosity of a man who would exploit the answer into a tall tale, but with the gentle concern of a friend.

Suddenly Zeb's eyes went dark again, as he remembered the cabin, the flames, the dirt in his mouth, Patience's body, and little Isaac. He clenched his fists and wanted a drink for the first time in a long time. "They killed my Patience. Killed my baby." It was said almost to himself, not in response to Jeremiah's question.

Both men stared out into the interior of the fort, keeping their own counsel. Jeremiah asked, quiet-like, "Is that why you went on the rampage, killin' all them Indians?"

"A course it is! Dirty redskins!" The tears that had been locked away for so long threatened at long last to spill out of his eyes and down his cheeks.

"Zeb, we been friends for a long, long time. Have you ever told anyone what happened?"

"No." It was almost a whisper.

"Do you want to tell me?"

One tear slipped out of his right eye as Zeb swallowed hard. The image of Patience's delicate, lovely body jumped unbidden into his mind. Without being able to stop himself, he replayed that awful morning again. He saw himself searching for a shovel, finding the spot where the Lady Slippers grew, digging the grave. He lingered over wrapping her body in the blanket, sobbed involuntarily as the blanket covered her beautiful face, obscuring her soft hair, hiding her tender lips, her cheeks once so healthy now cold and pale. He remembered placing her gently in the ground. He recalled gathering tiny baby Isaac tenderly to him, placing him on his mother's breast, trying to pray. More tears fell as he recalled the first shovel full of earth, more as the grave filled in. He remembered almost not being able to cover Patience's face with the soil, knowing it was over, done, finished. He would never see her again. He remembered searching for a suitable marker for the grave. And then the anger washed over him again and he felt the old rage whispering around the edges of his mind, sucking him in, seducing him with its tantalizing power to command his life.

He hadn't realized he had been recalling that awful day out loud until Jeremiah spoke. "How did they die, Zeb?"

With an effort, Zeb pushed back the rage. For reasons he didn't understand, he didn't want to throw himself over the cliff into despair. Not again. He'd been there before and, while it had driven him like a slave master to hunt and kill Indians, it left him gnawed and empty. Today, with Jeremiah sitting next to him on Ole' Aunt Betsy's porch and the thin sunlight warming him through the bare trees, he struggled to make the effort to step away from the edge of anger that had driven him for the past year.

"It was Injuns," he said. "Burnt the cabin, killed Patience and baby Isaac."

"How did you escape, Zeb?"

He sobbed again — the question cut too deep. "I don't rightly know. When I came to, I was lyin' face down in the dirt in front of the cabin."

"You weren't in the cabin? Did they club you or try to scalp you? Did you fight 'em?"

"Naw, they wasn't a mark on me. I felt for my scalp an' it was there. Didn't notice any blood or beat places. Didn't see any on Patience, either. I looked at her one last time — you know, before I laid her in the ground."

"That don't quite seem right, Zeb. Surely they'd 'a knocked you cold or somethin'."

There was the tiniest bit of familiarity to that thought. Had Zeb himself wondered that before?

"How did you know it was Indians, Zeb?" Jeremiah asked.

It came back in a flash. "Arrow," he said. "Broken Shawnee arrow, lying on the ground near the cabin."

"A broken arrow?"

"Yeah, a broken arrow with a yellow flint head. Triangular-like. You know, like we used to find ... "

"Used to find up on the mound when we were young boys?"

"Yeah, like those ..."

"Zeb, did that arrowhead have a chip of one side ..."

"... Yeah ..."

"And a white streak through the flint on the other side?"

Zeb closed his eyes. An ancient memory, from his childhood, was trying to surface. He couldn't quite remember ...

"Remember when we found them arrowheads, Zeb? Up on the Indian mound? Remember we found several, and you 'specially wanted to keep ..."

"The yellow one, with the white streak in it," Zeb finished. "Yes. Yes, I remember that arrowhead. An' you kep' the lighter colored one."

"That's right. And we mounted them on arrows and practiced shooting with bows we made."

"Yeah, I remember. What'd you do with your arrowhead, Jeremiah?"

Jeremiah reached inside his shirt and pulled out a thin leather thong. Tied to the end was a white arrowhead. "I keep it with me," he said. "'Cause we been friends for so long. What'd you do with your'n, Zeb?"

"I ... I don't rightly know. I ... I surely kep' it somewheres."

"I reckon you did, Zeb. Didn't you say that arrowhead you found after the cabin burnt was yellow, with a white streak in it?"

"Yeah, it did ..."

"With a chip out of the other side?"

"Yeah, but ..."

"Zeb, where'd you say your arrowhead was?"

Suddenly Zeb stood up. He was still stiff and his muscles groaned at the effort. "I gots to go, Jeremiah." He stepped down off the porch. "I'll be seeing you."

Jeremiah watched him go, pacing off across the interior of the fort toward the opening in the outer stockade. "Lord," he whispered, "my friend Zeb needs You to open his eyes. But open 'em gentle-like — he ain't real strong yet. But You need to show him what he done and what he needs to do."

A week or so later Jeremiah was cleaning his gun by the firelight. It has been a good few days of hunting. He became aware that someone was standing nearby. "Jeremiah, I need to ast you a question." It was Zeb.

"Sure, Zeb. Pull up a stool and set a spell."

Zeb squatted down on an up-turned log. Jeremiah continued cleaning his gun.

"The other day, when we was talking on Ole' Aunt Betsy's porch ... do you think that arrowhead I found was the one we found as boys, and not a Shawnee arrow from the raiding party?"

"What do you think, Zeb? You're the one that saw it, not me."

Zeb stared into the firelight. Finally he said, "I think it was the same arrowhead. I'm almost for shore."

"Me too, Zeb."

"Then that means ... that means ... I don't know what it means."

"What other sign was there, Zeb, that it was Shawnee what burnt your cabin?"

"That's just it, Jeremiah. I cain't rightly think of any other reason." A log on the fire settled and sparks flew up into the night. "I was so angry about Patience and baby Isaac that I didn't ..."

They sat in silence, the only sounds were the hissing of the fire and the soft rubbing sound of Jeremiah's cloth cleaning the gun.

"Do you remember anything that happened before that, Zeb? Anything at all?"

Elbows on his knees, Zeb laid his head in his hands, pressing his eyes against the heels of his palms. "I don't know. I jus' don't remember a thing."

The gun was clean enough, but Jeremiah kept on rubbing trying to make the gun perfect and giving Zeb time to think.

"Do you remember anything you were doing the day before? Did anyone come by the cabin? Did you go anywheres?"

"No, I ... I think I may have rode down to Jubal Bryan's place. I don't rightly know. It just don't come back to me that easy."

"Jubal Bryan. He lives in a cabin up on Red Lick don't he?"

"That's right. Up past Malory Springs."

"Don't Jude Isaacs live up that way, too?"

"Jude Isaacs ... Jude Isaacs. I hadn't a'thought a him in a long time. Jude Isaacs ..." Head still in his hands, Zeb spoke to the floor, almost in a whisper. But images, long hidden, were fading through the blackness, and he could see, like the edge of a mountain coming clear in the beginning light as dawn eased up on you after a long night. Jude Isaacs ... Jude made moonshine whiskey from corn he grew in a big old copper still he had trucked in from Virginia. He remembered going to see Jude, remembered trading with him.

"I don't remember," he whispered to Jeremiah. But he did. Like mountains in first light, the images were very pale and shadowy, barely distinguishable from the darkness all around, but, like the dawn coming from the East, there was no stopping the light, once it had begun, and soon more memories were surfacing.

Zeb pushed them back. He looked straight at Jeremiah. "I don't remember a thing."

Jeremiah placed the butt of the gun on the floor and held the barrel as if it were a staff. "You don't remember anything at all?"

"No." His voice was too emphatic.
"Nothing. Did I ever tell you what happened
when the Injuns captured me?"

"No, you didn't Zeb. I'd be glad to listen,
if'n you want to tell me."

So Zeb told him. Told him about the
Indian's he'd come upon, about lying on the rock
outcropping and plotting how he was going to
take all three of them. Told about being
ambushed by more Indians and being captured.
Told about being forced North, across the Ohio
to Chillicothe. Told about being tied to a stake.

"Did they torture you or mistreat you?"
asked Jeremiah.

"No ... no I can't rightly say that they did.
They fed me and gave me water. They didn't
beat me or anything. Just made me stand there,
tied to a stake."

He paused, remembering that day.

"They had some kind of trial. The big chief
was there, and he talked a lot. And he had
different braves, seven of 'em, talk. Each one
pointed to me. I knew they were sayin' I killed a
bunch of Indians. And I did! I never denied it!
They killed Patience and it was revenge, pure
and simple."

"So how did you get away, Zeb?"

"Well now, that's the part I don't
understand. I just don't understand it a'tall."
He looked across at Jeremiah, seeing the

firelight play shadows and light across his face. "This Indian brave ... I don't know who he was and never saw him before, 'cept ... well, he stepped up and talked a long time to the chief. I don't know what he was saying, but it was clear it made the chief sad. There was a tear on the old chief's face I could see in the firelight. Whatever was said, they suddenly let me go."

"Let you go?" Jeremiah was incredulous. Indians didn't let white men go.

"That's what I said. They let me go. Somehow that brave took my place."

"What do you mean, took your place? That don't make sense, Zeb."

"I know, I know! Hit don't make a lick a sense. It seems like as if they was goin' to torture me, hang me on some kind of contraption up in the air 'till I was dead. But, somehow, the Injun' took my place."

"But you killed a bunch a Indians, didn't you, Zeb? I mean, in a way, it woulda been within their right to string you up, wouldn't it?"

"Well ... well, yes, I reckon. I 'spect that would be so. 'Cept ... 'cept for what they done to Patience and Isaac." Suddenly, without warning, the image of Jude Isaacs came crashing into his memory. He couldn't prevent the memories, so long suppressed, from coming back. He remembered riding down Red Lick to Jude's place. Remembered trading him for some

corn liquor. Remembered sitting and drinking
with Jude, as he'd done before. Remembered
getting staggering drunk. Remembered climbing
on his horse, really too far gone to ride, falling
off and having to walk home, leaning against the
horse's flank, carrying a jug of moonshine in the
other.

"I got to get home," he said suddenly.

The next day Ole' Aunt Betsy begged him
to stay, said he wasn't strong enough yet. But,
with grim resolve, Zeb set off for the site of his
cabin. The settlers at Boonesboro set him up
with a few tools — an axe, a blanket, a flint and
steel — but Zeb didn't need much. He'd grown
used to living off the land, keeping his own
company.

When he first edged out of the woods into
the clearing where the burned out cabin lay, Zeb
almost thought he couldn't do it. But he was
able to reach deep down inside himself and find
the courage, the strength to go on. He paid his
respects at Patience and baby Isaac's grave, now
grown over with a fresh crop of Lady Slippers.
He built himself a little shelter and a fire pit to
cook over. He trapped rabbit and squirrel to eat.
Gradually he began clearing away the burned
logs, assessing the damage to the chimney,
resetting the foundation. At night he slept in the
shelter and, as the spring blossomed into
warmer weather, out in the open. He felled trees

with his borrowed axe and began the hard, sweaty work of rebuilding.

About mid day, as the walls of the cabin were starting to take shape, he heard a horse whinny down the path. Never a particularly fearful man, Zeb simply stood with the axe in his hand, his only real weapon. But it turned out to be Jude Isaacs, riding on his old roan, carrying a jug. That was Jude. If he ever came off of Red Lick, it was on his old roan. And he never went anywhere without his jug.

"'Zat you, Zeb Tate?" he called.

"Is that you, Jude Isaacs?"

"Why, it shore is me, I'll be dogged. Has been all day!" He pulled up the horse at the cabin wall and flipped the reins onto a stob that hadn't been fully trimmed yet. "I heard you was home, Zeb."

He dismounted.

"Yeah, I reckon I'm home." But was this home? Would he really be able to live here?

"I heard you was off huntin' Injuns."

"I was. But I'm not now."

"I see that." Jude cast an appraising eye over the cabin taking shape. "Buildin' her back, I see."

A crow called from the top of a sycamore tree down by the spring. Another answered from farther back in the woods.

"I brung you something. Hit'll do you good." Jude held out the jug toward Zeb. "Welcome home."

"Hit'll do me good? Hit'll do me good?" Zeb looked up at Jude. Those words ...

"Shore it will! Hit's good for what's in you." He uncorked the jug and the cloying, astringent scent of the moonshine reached out and tickled Zeb's nose. "Here, let's drink to you comin' home!"

"Hit'll do me good? Truly, Jude? I ... I don't rightly think it will."

The memory of staggering home to Patience from a night of drinking with Jude came again. He remembered Patience meeting him at the door. Remembered the disappointment in her face. Remembered ... remembered raising his hand to her and putting her in her place. How dare she question him? Remembered the fire in the chimney. Remembered the chinking she'd been after him to fix. Remembered ... he didn't want to remember any more.

He looked over at the chimney. There it was, as plain as day. Why hadn't he seen it before? The missing chinking, the black charring radiating out. He was the one who hadn't done his job. He was the one who hadn't protected his family.

He sank down on his knees in the dirt of the cabin, right where he had found Patience's body that awful morning. "Oh, it was me!" he sobbed. "It was me!" He tore his clothes in anguish, pulled out handfuls of hair. "Oh Lord, it was me!"

"Here now, Zeb. Git a'hold a' yerself! Ain't no need to go on thataway. Here. Take a pull on this corn. That's what you need." He held the jug so close to Zeb that Zeb could hear the liquor sloshing around inside.

Part of him desperately wanted to reach out his hand, take the jug, take a long, long drink. The thirst in him was powerful, rampaging, furious. He wanted to pitch himself over into oblivion, to forget, to numb the pain that was so much a part of him. But there was another force within him, too. A force that fought against despair, that looked hard into his soul, into who Zeb Tate really was, and showed him he could be a different man, that he could overcome.

The tears were streaming down Zeb's face. The reality of who had really killed Patience and their baby broke him completely. There was nothing left. Except ... Except for piercing black eyes that, for reasons that made no sense at all, had known him in an unknowable way.

Zeb slapped the jug away from him, almost causing Jude to drop it. "Hey!" he protested.

"Get away from me!" Zeb stood up and the power emanated from his demeanor. Jude involuntarily backed away a step. "Get away from me, Jude Isaacs, and never come back!"

"Now, Zeb," Jude said in a voice that almost sounded like he was whining. "You always did like a little 'shine. I brung you some, real peaceful and friendly like. No need to act like that."

"I'm a'tellin' you, Jude. Get away. Take yer jug and go back to Red Lick. You ain't welcome here." He picked up the axe and shouldered it meaningfully.

"Now Zeb. You ain't thinkin'. You'll come to yer senses and want me back. I'll ... I'll just be moseying along now. But I'll be back."

"No Jude. You take your jug and you light out of here. And don't you never, never ever come back!"

Jude got the message, mounted his horse, and headed down the path.

Zeb did not instantly become a new man. He was still the same Zeb: a loner, a bit of an outcast, given to a quick temper. But something inside him that day, seeing the chimney and recognizing how wrong he'd been about the fire and what caused it, about Patience and baby Isaac, something inside him broke. Broke and reformed into a new configuration.

He lost interest in rebuilding the cabin. It was just too painful. He drifted up to Boonesboro again. Ole' Aunt Betsy allowed him to squat at her cabin. He spent more time with Jeremiah, sitting on the porch steps, watching the days ripen into full summer, listening to the mocking birds in the treetops, watching the bright red of the cardinals against the dark green of the hemlocks and rhododendron. And then he found himself heading north. He didn't rightly know why, but it seemed like the thing to do. He was just as comfortable sleeping out in the open as he was in Ole' Aunt Betsy's cabin. His own company was adequate. And so he walked north until he reached the banks of the Ohio.

There, tucked under some overhanging maples, were three canoes, right where he thought they'd be. He eased one out into the water, first paddling upstream, but then changing his mind and heading down. He saw the great sycamore tree, leaning out over the water, its mottled bark forming a comfortable pattern of lights and darks. He steered towards it. Then he saw the man he expected to see lying on the trunk out over the water. There was no need for the man to reach out his hand; it was a simple matter for Zeb to paddle to the bank and jump out, securing the canoe to a small gum.

The Indian scrambled down out of the great tree and stood gazing at Zeb with those piercing black eyes. The animosity in Zeb's heart was gone, although he would not have said that enduring the scrutiny of those eyes was exactly comfortable or easy.

The Indian spoke. "Come," he said. "We go."

And Zeb followed.

Think on These Things

1. Was the ending of the story a surprise or did you see it coming? What elements in the story foreshadowed the ending?

2. What do you think is the major theme of this story? If you could summarize "Frontier Life" in just one or a few words, what word or words would you use? Support your answer with reasons.

3. There are several places in the story that Zeb's living conditions change dramatically. Some of the places are early in the story, in the middle of the story, and towards the end. Make a list of the key places in the plot where Zeb's status changes. Which of these is most important and why?

4. Are there places in the story where there is a change, not so much based on Zeb's external conditions, but based on Zeb's internal decisions? What are those places? Discuss the significance of each of Zeb's major decision-points.

5. There are several white settlers in the story that assist Zeb. Who are those settlers? What roles did they play in Zeb's recovery after being captured?

6. What did you think about what happened in Chillicothe? Did it add to the drama of the story, or was it too unrealistic? What thoughts and emotions did you have about the events that led to Zeb's being set free?

7. What emotions do you think the old chief had as he set Zeb free? What do you think was going through his mind? Why do you think that?

8. Find the place in the story where a crow calls. What do you think this symbolizes?

9. Discuss the role of Jude Issacs in the story. Are there parallels you can draw between Jude Issacs and characters in other stories you've read?

10. Contrast the three Indian braves in the story — the one in Zeb's dream at the beginning, the one who took Zeb's place at Chillicothe, and the one at the end of the story in the tree. What differences do you see between them? What similarities do they share? What is Zeb's relationship to each one as they appear in the story?

11. Can you think of examples from history where one person has given his life in exchange for another's? How unusual is that? How much more unusual would it be if the person who was the beneficiary was a sworn enemy of the person giving up his life? What could possibly have motivated the Indian brave to have made the sacrifice he made?

12. Is there anything for which you would give up your life? If there is, what it and why would you be willing to do so? If not, why not? Is there anyone who would give up their life to

save you? If so, who would that be, and why would they be willing to do so?

To purchase additional copies of this book, contact us at Narrow Gate House Publishers:

www.NarrowGateHouse.com

www.ingramcontent.com/pod-product-compliance
Lightning Source LLC
Chambersburg PA
CBHW031256090426
42742CB00007B/480